WHAT CONTENT-AREA TEACHERS SHOULD KNOW ABOUT ADOLESCENT LITERACY

EDUCATION IN A COMPETITIVE
AND GLOBALIZING WORLD SERIES

Success in Mathematics Education
Caroline B. Baumann
2009. ISBN: 978-1-60692-299-6

Mentoring: Program Development, Relationships and Outcomes
Michael I. Keel (Editor)
2009. ISBN: 978-1-60692-287-3

Mentoring: Program Development, Relationships and Outcomes
Michael I. Keel (Editor)
2009. ISBN: 978-1-60876-727-4
(Online Book)

Motivation in Education
Desmond H. Elsworth (Editor)
2009. ISBN: 978-1-60692-234-7

Evaluating Online Learning: Challenges and Strategies for Success
Arthur T. Weston (Editor)
2009. ISBN: 978-1-60741-107-9

Enhancing Prospects of Longer-Term Sustainability of Cross-Cultural INSET Initiatives in China
Chunmei Yan
2009. ISBN: 978-1-60741-615-9

Reading at Risk: A Survey of Literary Reading in America
Rainer D. Ivanov
2009. ISBN: 978-1-60692-582-9

Reading: Assessment, Comprehension and Teaching
Nancy H. Salas and Donna D. Peyton (Editors)
2009. ISBN: 978-1-60692-615-4

Reading: Assessment, Comprehension and Teaching
Nancy H. Salas and Donna D. Peyton (Editors)
2009. ISBN: 978-1-60876-543-0
(Online Book)

Multimedia in Education and Special Education
Onan Demir and Cari Celik
2009. ISBN: 978-1-60741-073-7

Rural Education in the 21st Century
Christine M.E. Frisiras (Editor)
2009. ISBN: 978-1-60692-966-7

Nutrition Education and Change
Beatra F. Realine (Editor)
2009. ISBN: 978-1-60692-983-4

Sexuality Education

Kelly N. Stanton

2010. ISBN: 978-1-60876-465-5

Sexuality Education and Attitudes

Jovan Stanovic and Milo Lalic
(Editors)

2010. ISBN: 978-1-60741-662-3

What Content-Area Teachers Should Know About Adolescent Literacy

National Institute for Literacy

2010. ISBN 978-1-60741-137-6

EDUCATION IN A COMPETITIVE AND GLOBALIZING WORLD SERIES

WHAT CONTENT-AREA TEACHERS SHOULD KNOW ABOUT ADOLESCENT LITERACY

NATIONAL INSTITUTE FOR LITERACY

Nova Science Publishers, Inc.

New York

NOTICE TO THE READER

The Publisher has taken reasonable care in the preparation of this book, but makes no expressed or implied warranty of any kind and assumes no responsibility for any errors or omissions. No liability is assumed for incidental or consequential damages in connection with or arising out of information contained in this book. The Publisher shall not be liable for any special, consequential, or exemplary damages resulting, in whole or in part, from the readers' use of, or reliance upon, this material. Any parts of this book based on government reports are so indicated and copyright is claimed for those parts to the extent applicable to compilations of such works.

Independent verification should be sought for any data, advice or recommendations contained in this book. In addition, no responsibility is assumed by the publisher for any injury and/or damage to persons or property arising from any methods, products, instructions, ideas or otherwise contained in this publication.

This publication is designed to provide accurate and authoritative information with regard to the subject matter covered herein. It is sold with the clear understanding that the Publisher is not engaged in rendering legal or any other professional services. If legal or any other expert assistance is required, the services of a competent person should be sought. FROM A DECLARATION OF PARTICIPANTS JOINTLY ADOPTED BY A COMMITTEE OF THE AMERICAN BAR ASSOCIATION AND A COMMITTEE OF PUBLISHERS.

LIBRARY OF CONGRESS CATALOGING-IN-PUBLICATION DATA

What content-area teachers should know about adolescent literacy / National Institute for Literacy.
    p. cm.
Includes bibliographical references and index.
ISBN 978-1-60741-137-6 (softcover)
1. Reading (Secondary)--United States. 2. Content area reading--United States. I. National Institute for Literacy (U.S.)
  LB1632.W46 2009
  428.4071'2--dc21
                        2009028470

Published by Nova Science Publishers, Inc. ✛ *New York*

CONTENTS

x   Contents

PREFACE

The goal of this book is to help address middle and high school classroom teachers', administrators', and parents' immediate need for basic information about how to build adolescents' reading and writing skills. The National Institute of Child Health and Human Development, the U.S. Department of Education, and other organizations currently sponsor long-term research studies that ultimately will add to our knowledge of adolescent literacy. In the meantime, however, the need for information to use in the classroom must be met.

This book summarizes some of the current literature on adolescent literacy research and practice. It is not a research synthesis or a literature review; such an effort is well beyond the scope of this document. Rather the book suggests some methods of building adolescent reading and writing skills in the classroom. To the extent possible, recommendations are evidence-based. There is little published literature on the effectiveness of instructional approaches or programs for adolescents, and the results from some new effectiveness research, now in press, were not available during the development of this book. With the limited research base available, research on other groups such as younger readers, dyslexic readers, and adult beginning readers have informed the recommendations made in this document. Extrapolating from this research does not negate the need or import of research investigating the effectiveness of instructional approaches or programs for adolescent, but rather provides useful guidance that can inform what instructors do today.

This book is a revision of the 2006 Preview Copy *What Content-Area Teachers Should Know About Adolescent Literacy.* There has been some new work in adolescent literacy published since the Preview Copy was released and these important publications have been included in the Additional References section.

An interagency working group, composed of representatives from the National Institute for Literacy, the U.S. Department of Education's Office of Adult and Vocational Education, and the National Institute of Child Health and Human Development, oversaw the development of the summary. The working group used *The National Reading Panel* report (NRP) [1] as background material to guide the organization of topics and shape the topic area search terms. The basic areas of reading (phonological processes, that is, the sound system, morphology, fluency, vocabulary and reading comprehension) form the core of the summary, with adjustments to accommodate differences in the middle and high school population addressed. The NRP report dealt predominantly with elementary grade readers. The book adds findings from the literature on topics relevant to adolescent readers, such as writing, morphological skills and motivation for reading. The book also includes a section on reading assessment and monitoring, even though little literature is available specifically on assessment and monitoring of adolescent readers. However, teachers need to assess and monitor their middle and high school students to determine whether or not a practice is effective for students in their specific classrooms.

Two major sources informed the working groups' development of a search process for source documents for this paper: Cooper's (1998) *Synthesizing Research: A Guide for Literature Review* [2]; and Creswell's (2003) *Research Design: Qualitative, Quantitative, and Mixed Methods Approaches* [3]. To identify relevant literature, the National Library of Education conducted searches based on the search terms "adolescent literacy," "adolescent readers," "reading in the content areas," and "comprehension strategies for high school" using the ISI Web of Science, Education Abstracts, and EBSCO Academic Search Premier databases. Searches were also conducted on PSYCH INFO and ERIC electronic databases using the topic area search terms.

Based on these searches the adolescent literacy interagency working group selected a list of suggested source documents. To the greatest degree possible, sources were selected that used scientifically-based research methods. Scientifically-based research involves the application of rigorous, systematic, and objective procedures to obtain reliable and valid knowledge relevant to education activities and programs [4].

The sources summarized in the book are included in the reference section. Additional peer-reviewed publications, summary books, and book chapters (some in press), provided background information and are noted by an asterisk.* It is important to note that a few key documents have been published since the preview edition of this document and allow for a more thorough understanding of the academic research on adolescent literacy. These documents are listed in the resource section of this book.

INTRODUCTION

Adolescents entering the adult world in the 21st century will read and write more than at any other time in human history. They will need advanced levels of literacy to perform their jobs, run their households, act as citizens, and conduct their personal lives. They will need literacy to cope with the flood of information they will find everywhere they turn. They will need literacy to feed their imagination so they can create the world of the future [5].

Despite the call for today's adolescents to achieve higher levels of literacy than previous generations, approximately 8.7 million fourth through twelfth grade students struggle with the reading and writing tasks that are required of them in school [6]. For many adolescent students, ongoing difficulties with reading and writing figure prominently in the decision to drop out of school [7]. These indicators suggest that literacy instruction should continue beyond the elementary years and should be tailored to the more complex forms of literacy that are required of adolescent students in the middle and high school years.

A growing research base on adolescent literacy supports an emphasis on direct instruction in the reading and writing skills needed to perform these more complex literacy tasks. However, many middle and high school teachers have little or no preparation for teaching these skills within their content-area disciplines and have few resources upon which to draw when they are faced with students whose academic reading and writing skills do not match their expectations [8]. Given this, it is important to realize that the responsibilities for strengthening literacy skills in these students is the responsibility of everyone at the school ranging from the language-arts instructors, reading specialists, content-area teachers, speech and hearing specialists, school psychologists, administrators, and others. The roles will likely be different for individuals in each of these groups, but everyone can take concrete steps to better identify adolescents that are struggling and address their literacy needs. The purpose of this resource document is to summarize and discuss the most recent adolescent literacy research and to describe promising, research-based instructional practices that can improve adolescents' academic reading and writing skills.

This document provides more general information for content-area teachers so that they will gain a deeper understanding of the underlying skills their students will need and the kind of instruction needed to develop these skills. Armed with this knowledge, we hope teachers will seek out the assistance struggling readers and writers need and be able to support the literacy skills of all students in the classrooms by incorporating some of these practices and strategies into their own content-focused instruction.

This book is divided into two main sections. The first section describes five key components that are critical to the development of reading proficiency: decoding/phonemic awareness and phonics, morphology, vocabulary, fluency, and text comprehension. Although much of the research on these five components was conducted with beginning readers, evidence gathered for this book suggests that the degree to which individuals have mastered the skills and abilities associated with these components affects their reading ability in later years. Thus, the first section focuses on five components of reading so as to help middle and high school teachers understand the skills and abilities mastered by good readers and the challenges faced by struggling readers, and provide illustrations of research-based instructional practices.

The second section discusses four other areas that are fundamental in helping adolescents achieve advanced levels of literacy: assessment, writing, motivation, and the needs of diverse learners. First, it is important that teachers gain insight into how reading assessment can be used to identify specific strengths and weaknesses related to students' reading abilities. Second, in addition to attaining high levels of reading proficiency, adolescents must become skilled writers capable of communicating information and ideas in a variety of forms and for a variety of purposes. Because writing style and purpose vary across different academic disciplines, contentarea teachers must be able to teach students how to write using the text structures and stylistic conventions that are prevalent in their disciplines. Third, struggling readers are often less motivated to read than successful readers; therefore, teachers must understand how they can influence student motivation for reading. Finally, because adolescents come from diverse cultural, linguistic, and socioeconomic backgrounds, special consideration needs to be given to the differentiated instruction necessary to meet the needs of diverse learners. Instruction in key literacy components combined with the ongoing use of reading assessment, instruction in writing, the use of strategies for building motivation, and attending to the needs of diverse learners provides a foundation for addressing the complex literacy learning needs of all adolescent students.

This document should not be considered a comprehensive guide to addressing the instructional needs of struggling adolescent readers but should be utilized as a resource for teachers who seek evidence-based strategies for teaching students to read and write texts that are characteristic of content-area disciplines.

KEY LITERACY COMPONENTS

Research has shown that *what you teach* and the *amount of time* you spend teaching it account for the greatest variance in student achievement [8]. Although developing a school-wide approach that addresses the *amount of time* needed for literacy instruction across the curriculum is beyond the scope of this book, teachers working within content-area departments or gradelevel teams can collaborate and share responsibility for integrating literacy instructional activities into their individual classes. Teachers can discuss the ideas and instructional strategies that are presented in this book with their colleagues and develop ways to coordinate integration of the strategies across classrooms and content areas.

This section of the book focuses on *"what you teach,"* or the content of literacy instruction in middle and high school. The following key literacy components are addressed: decoding/phonemic awareness and phonics, morphology, vocabulary, fluency, and text comprehension. Each section provides the following information for the component being addressed: a description of the literacy component, an explanation of how good readers approach it, a discussion of the challenges faced by adolescents in learning the associated skills and strategies, recommended instructional techniques for addressing literacy in content-area classrooms, and examples of research areas that still need to be explored.

All of the literacy components are important aspects of skilled reading, but some of the components described below are most feasibly taught by reading specialists rather than within the context of content-area courses. In particular, the recommendations concerning decoding are not intended to suggest that content-area teachers focus on developing those skills in contentarea classrooms. Although all teachers share responsibilities for the literacy development of their students, students with difficulties in decoding will need more intensive intervention than is possible within a content-area class. Rather, the information presented here is intended to help content-area instructors become more aware of the literacy skills that skilled readers possess and recognize when students struggle with these foundational skills. These students and others identified as struggling in reading should be referred to a reading specialist for more formal assessment to gain a better understanding of their literacy skills.

DECODING

Decoding or word identification refers to the ability to correctly decipher a particular word out of a group of letters. Two of the skills involved in decoding or word identification are *phonemic awareness* and *phonics. Phonemic awareness* is the understanding that spoken words are made up of individual units of sound. These units of sound are called phonemes [6, 9]. Adolescents who are phonemically aware, for example, understand that three phonemes, /k/, /a/, and /t/, form the word cat. Students understand that the word *fish* also has three phonemes because *s* and *h* together make the distinct sound, /sh/. Phonemic awareness also includes the ability to identify and manipulate these individual units of sound [6, 9]. For example, phonemically aware students can make a new word out of *weather* by removing and replacing the first consonant sound with another consonant sound (e.g., *feather*).

According to the National Reading Panel report [1], direct instruction in phonemic awareness is most beneficial when offered to young children. Kamil (2003) [6] arrived at similar conclusions in his review of the literature, stating that phonemic awareness instruction is most effective in supporting reading improvement if it is provided in kindergarten and first grade. In fact, most children gather some level of awareness of phonemes before their adolescent years. If this awareness has not been fully developed and exercised, however, middle and high school students may experience difficulty with phonemic awareness when they encounter words that are unfamiliar to them. Research has found that instruction in decoding, word recognition, and spelling help improve phonemic awareness for students who have difficulty understanding how to blend sounds to articulate unfamiliar words [1, 6, 9].

Phonics is the understanding of the relationship between the letters in written words and the sounds of these words when spoken [1]. Students use this understanding as the basis for learning to read and write. Phonics helps students to recognize familiar words and decode new ones, providing these students a predictable, rules-based system for reading [1, 6, 10].

What Do Good Readers Do?

Good readers have a conscious understanding of the individual sounds, or *phonemes*, within spoken words and how these sounds are manipulated to form words [9]. In a spoken word, phonemes are the smallest parts of sound that make a difference in meaning. For example, changing the first phoneme in the word *map* from /m/ to /k/ changes the word from *map* to *cap*. Successful readers manipulate the blending and segmentation of phonemes used in speech and use this knowledge to support their ability to read new words and to learn to spell words. Adolescent readers make many of these sound connections at the syllable level and decode new sounds using word chunks or syllables, such as *re-*, *pro-*, *-tion*, *-ment*, that are already familiar to them [11].

Readers with strong phonics skills are able to use their knowledge of letters and their sounds to pronounce unknown words. This ability allows readers to listen to the pronunciation of an unknown word and match the pronounced word to one that they recognize in their *receptive* (listening) and *productive* (speaking) vocabularies. Readers with strong phonics skills rely on these skills to decode quickly unknown words that they encounter while reading [6, 10, 11].

What Challenges Do Adolescent Readers Face Regarding Decoding?

Content-area teachers need to be aware of the literacy challenges faced by adolescent readers with decoding problems. These struggling readers need more intensive intervention in order to remediate their reading difficulties. To provide some perspective on the scope of the problem, some researchers estimate that approximately 10% of adolescents struggle with word identification skills [16-18]. Although this percentage may not seem that large on the surface, it is important to realize that this estimate is for the population of all adolescents and that when talking specifically about struggling readers this estimate is likely to be much higher [19]; with this in mind, reading or literacy specialists, together with others in their schools, serve as an important resource to more systematically address the needs of these students. This section aims to provide some useful background for content-area teachers regarding the challenges faced by adolescent readers struggling with decoding skills.

Based on their research, Shaywitz et al. (1999) [12] asserted that students who are unsuccessful in reading words that are unfamiliar to them may also struggle with poor phonemic awareness skills. This is especially problematic for adolescent readers with dyslexia and those who encounter many words that are new to them as they read content-area texts. Studies involving adolescents with dyslexia have revealed that an individual's lack of phonemic awareness represents the specific cognitive deficit responsible for dyslexia [10, 13-15]. Without sufficient awareness of the sounds that make these new words, adolescent readers are unable to move to other levels of literacy, such as phonics or fluency. More simply put, phonemic awareness has been found to mediate word identification in all readers; therefore, this phonological skill deserves the attention of educators in middle and high schools.

Struggling with phonics negatively affects students' reading comprehension skills, vocabulary knowledge, and reading fluency. Adolescents with weak phonics skills lack effective strategies for decoding unknown multi-syllabic words. Even words used by students when conversing with others can be the same words these students are unable to sound out when presented with the words in print. As a result, these words remain unknown to them in print [6, 10, 16, 18]. At grade five and beyond, students encounter 10,000 or more new words a year in their grade-level and content-area texts, and most of these words are multi-syllabic [20]. Not surprisingly, the inability to decode multi-syllabic words negatively influences readers' comprehension. Readers whose poor phonics skills prevent them from reading grade-level text independently cannot build their reading vocabularies at the same rate as their peers.

How can Instruction Help Adolescent Students with Decoding?

Adolescents with decoding difficulties need more intensive practice and instructional time to develop their reading skills more thoroughly. Specifically decoding instruction should emphasize syllable patterns and morphology. This instruction would be, in general, most appropriately delivered by a reading specialist, and content-area instructors should focus on referring adolescent students with difficulties in phonemic awareness and/or phonics to a reading specialist for formal assessment of their reading skills. The following section focuses on instructional approaches that can strengthen phonics and phonemic awareness skills and provides examples on how they can be incorporated into classroom instruction.

For struggling adolescent students with decoding difficulties, the reading specialist should integrate phonemic awareness and phonics instruction as a support to the classroom lessons and texts that are assigned. Although there is little research on adolescents and phonemic awareness, recommendations for instructing adolescent students who struggle with phonemic awareness and phonics can be derived from research involving students with dyslexia [10, 12-15] and adult beginning readers [21-23].

Both phonics and phonemic awareness instruction should occur within the context of an integrated approach to developing students' comprehension and use of academic language (that is, the language used in educational settings) and should focus on only one or two skills or strategies at a time [1]. Important components of academic language are the vocabulary used to communicate concepts within a particular discipline (specialized academic vocabulary such as *osmosis* and *perimeter*) and the vocabulary used across disciplines to express precisely ideas and information (non-specialized academic vocabulary such as *examine* and *cause*). Academic vocabulary is distinguished from the "everyday" vocabulary that is used to communicate on a less formal level outside of the classroom [24, 25]. For example, the non-specialized academic vocabulary words *examine* and *cause* contrast with the everyday vocabulary words *look at* and *make*.

The following research-based recommendations provide context for how phonemic awareness and phonics instruction can be directly taught to explicitly build these skills or primarily aimed at strengthening these skills by incorporating them into activities that also build other literacy components such as vocabulary. It is not envisioned that content-area instructors will focus on these phonemic awareness and phonics skills during their instruction but it may help instructors gain a clearer sense of where struggling readers might have difficulties.

Modeling Phonemic Awareness Skills When Introducing New Vocabulary

Phonemic awareness skills can be strengthened through instruction when introducing new vocabulary. To develop these skills, the reading specialist should provide instruction with a focus on identification of rhyming words, blending of isolated sounds to form words, and segmentation of a word into its individual sounds [5, 12]. While this instruction is not intended to be delivered in the content-area classroom, it could be appropriate in the English language arts class. For example, when teaching the conventions of poetry, English language arts teachers can read aloud poems that rhyme and draw students' attention to the rhyming words. They can also ask students to identify the particular syllable or syllables within the words that are responsible for the rhyme.

Instruction can also emphasize specialized academic vocabulary for words that change meaning when one phoneme is substituted for another and emphasize these changes when introducing new vocabulary. For example, a teacher can demonstrate how deleting the phoneme /r/ from the word *revolution* results in the word *evolution* and likewise demonstrate how adding the phoneme /r/ to the word *evolution* results in the word *revolution*. Segmenting words into their phoneme units helps develop students' awareness of the relationship between sound and meaning. Follow-up discussion of the phonological and semantic similarities and differences between words such as *revolution* and *evolution* will help students not only develop phonological awareness but also extend their vocabulary knowledge [5, 12].

Providing Instruction in Phonics Strategies Helps Students Articulate and Identify Multi-syllabic Words

Research on phonics indicates that certain phonics instructional strategies improve the reading abilities of both younger and older readers [16, 26, 27]. Although research has suggested that phonics instruction is useful for all students [28], those with weak phonological skills tend to benefit most from this type of instruction [18, 29, 30].

Multi-syllabic words are especially important, as these words encompass most of the new vocabulary encountered by adolescents in their reading. Multi-syllabic words also provide much of the new information in content-area texts [6, 16, 20]. Teaching word analysis strategies for decoding multi-syllabic words helps adolescent readers decode other unknown words, build a sight-word vocabulary, and learn how to spell words [10, 18, 27].

When selecting vocabulary words to teach, teachers should focus on multi-syllabic, high frequency, specialized and non-specialized academic words and on sound patterns that are difficult for struggling readers. Examples of multi-syllabic words found in content-area reading are *circumference*, *geographical*, *parameter*, *imperative*, and *simultaneous*.

As mentioned earlier, for those students who continue to struggle with phonics and phonemic awareness skills, more focused instruction should primarily be delivered by reading specialists after the reading skills of these struggling students have been formally assessed and their areas of difficulties identified. Listed below are some suggested guidelines for how phonics instruction could be delivered for difficult academic vocabulary and sound patterns:

- Take time before lessons to determine the content-area words with which students may struggle.
- When introducing these words, articulate each syllable slowly (e.g., *e-co-sys-tem*), pausing slightly between the syllables [16, 17, 31]. Repeat this articulation several times.
- Point out patterns in the pronunciation and spelling of prefixes, suffixes, and vowels in selected words (e.g., *rac-ism, sex-ism, age-ism*, etc.) [11, 20].
- Point out similarities and differences among words that belong to "word families" (e.g., *define, definitely, definition*) [32].
- Model using new or difficult words in different contexts [16, 26, 33].
- Provide opportunities for students to practice using new or difficult words and reinforce correct pronunciation and usage [16, 26, 33].
- Ask open-ended questions that require students to respond using the new or difficult words (e.g., Do you think racism, sexism, or ageism is more prevalent in our society? Why?) [16, 26, 33].

Use Direct, Explicit, and Systematic Instruction to Teach Phonemic Awareness and Phonics Skills

Scientific research supports the use of direct, explicit, and systematic instruction for teaching phonemic awareness and phonics [6, 12, 16, 20, 34-36]. Examples of steps that could be used by teachers are listed below; however, note that for adolescent students this instruction is most appropriately delivered by a reading specialist rather than a content-area instructor:

1. Explain, demonstrate, and model the skill or strategy with content-area words and within the context of the subject matter students are currently learning.
2. Guide students to practice the skill or strategy and provide *corrective feedback* (or informing the student of their incorrect practice and giving them the correct information) [37].
3. Provide time for independent or peer-collaborative practice of the skill or strategy.

4. Repeat these instructional steps until students are able to apply the skill or strategy independently in their reading and writing [18, 29, 30].

As you may have noticed, teachers could take advantage of some of the suggestions above to introduce new vocabulary that their students may encounter in the content-area classes they teach. When introducing new vocabulary words that have common prefixes, suffixes, or roots, teachers can instruct students in the meanings of these word parts and how to use this knowledge to decipher new words. Teachers can begin with vocabulary that they are currently teaching and then extend instruction to non-specialized academic vocabulary and specialized vocabulary from other disciplines. For example, teachers can teach students the meaning of the prefix *poly* when teaching the words *polygon* and *polyhedron*. At the same time, they can teach students how to apply knowledge of these prefixes to decipher the meanings of other words that begin with the prefix (e.g., *polytheism, polygraph, polygamy,* etc.) [20].

Provide Extra Time for Phonemic Awareness and Phonics Instruction and Opportunities for Students to Practice Using New Skills When Reading

Adolescent readers who struggle with decoding need extra time to decode each word and to apply their higher order thinking skills to comprehend fully the text that they read [15]. These students will need extra time for reading in the classroom and outside of class. For adolescent students who struggle with decoding, they should be referred to the reading specialist on staff to more intensively address their reading needs. As an aid, content-area teachers may consider taping instructional lessons and passing on these tapes to struggling readers to review at their own pace [12].

What Do We Still Need to Know?

Much more research needs to be conducted with adolescent students in the areas of phonemic awareness and phonics. Investigation of students' phonological skills has typically occurred in the primary and elementary grades. With both young children and adolescents, however, there are still many questions that need to be answered. For example, research is needed to study whether or not small group settings are the most effective teaching environment for phonemic awareness for older students. In addition, researchers have paid little attention to the possible connections between phonics instruction and motivation. It is important to better understand how adolescents' levels of motivation influence their reading ability [1, 9, 26]. Finally, additional research is needed to determine how decoding and fluency skills relate to reading difficulties faced by some older students.

MORPHOLOGY

Morphology is the study of word structure [38, 39]. Morphology describes how words are formed from morphemes [38]. A morpheme is the smallest unit of meaning in a word. A morpheme may be as short as one letter such as the letter, 's'. This letter adds plurality to a word such as cats. Likewise, a morpheme can consist of letter combinations that contain meaning. These units of meaning could be roots, prefixes and suffixes. An example of a morpheme that consists of letter combinations would be the word pronoun. This is also a compound word. Several combinations of word types can be created by compounding words; however, it is important to point out to the student that the meaning of a compound word does not always match the meanings of the individual words separately [38].

Morphemes can be manipulated to modify the word structures in order to change the meaning of the word [38]. For example, "She bakes cookies", can be changed to "She baked cookies." In this example, the "s" that signifies plurality is changed to "ed" and is indicative of past tense. Here the meaning of the word changes as well as the meaning of the sentence.

Morphology does make a reliable independent contribution to both reading and writing [40]. The unique contribution of morphological awareness to literacy skills is evident in the decoding rate of students in grades 8 and 9, and importantly morphological learning is still developing in the late school-age years [39].

What Do Good Readers Do?

Students who understand words at the morphemic level are better able to get the meaning of words and are better prepared to deal with the increased reading and writing demands across the curriculum and content areas [41]. Good readers use their knowledge of morphological structure to recognize complex words [40].

What Challenges Do Adolescent Readers Face with Morphology?

Struggling adolescent readers who lack the knowledge of morphological structure will have more difficulty in recognizing and learning words. Research shows that this awareness of the morphological structure of words is correlated with students' vocabulary knowledge as well as their reading comprehension [40].

Students with language learning disabilities may experience difficulty with delayed vocabulary and difficulty in defining specific vocabulary words because of a deficit in their knowledge of morphology [38].

How Can Instruction Help Adolescent Students with Morphology?

When adolescent students learn frequently used morphemes this knowledge improves not only their spelling, but also provides strategies for decoding and for building vocabulary [42]. Learning morphemes helps students particularly in the upper elementary grades and beyond as they encounter more unfamiliar words and morphologically complex words across their expository textbooks and narrative literature as well as in spelling tasks[43]. Students with morphological knowledge are better able to separate out the morphemes into meaningful units for use in decoding, comprehending or spelling the word [43].

Teach Different Morpheme Patterns

When teaching new words, teachers should not only consider the spelling of the word, but also should explain the morphemes role in changing word meaning. It is important to teach the different morpheme patterns and although formal instruction in the different morpheme patterns is likely beyond the scope of a content-area instructor, these instructors could introduce the morpheme patterns that are related to the content vocabulary that they will need to teach in their class. For background purposes, there are several morpheme patterns that include: Anglo-Saxon morphemes, Latin morphemes, and Greek morphemes. Adolescent readers will benefit from learning these morpheme patterns.

The Anglo-Saxon words tend to be the first taught words in primary school [42]. These words tend to be common, everyday words that are found in primary grade text [42]. Examples of these words are: *cat, do, friend*, and *want*.

Latin words make up the majority of the words in English and are the words that are generally polysyllabic and found in the upper elementary and secondary literature as well as expository text. Words of Latin origin contain a root along with the addition of either a prefix and/or suffix [41]. Examples of these words are: *informing, conventional*, and *disrupted*.

Greek words form about 10% of the words we use and are found in students' science, math, and philosophy textbooks around the 3rd grade and beyond [41, 42, 44]. Words of Greek origin tend to consist of a combination of roots that are connected to make a word [41]. Examples of these words are: *chromosome, hydrogen, physiology* and *atmosphere*.

Bound morphemes are suffixes and prefixes. These morphological word endings are meaningful units only when attached to another morpheme that is the root word. Examples of these bound morphemes that would help students comprehend the words being taught are: *-ed, -ing, -s*, and *-'s* [38]. When bound morphemes are added to a word they can change the meaning of the word.

Free morphemes are another type of morpheme that can present difficulty for students. Free morphemes can stand alone as a word and do not have to be combined with other morphemes. An example of this type of morpheme is the word *man*. These particular morphemes are divided into content words and function words. Function words such as pronouns, conjunctions, prepositions, articles, and auxiliary verbs are learned early; however, these are often problematic for the student with language learning disabilities [38].

There are several recommended classroom activities that will help with the learning of morphology. Specifically these activities relate to the structural components of words plus relationships among words. Brice (2004) [38] suggests that general educators, special educators, and speech language pathologists all share the responsibility for teaching the following:

- Syllable types and syllable division,
- Base words, prefixes, and suffixes,
- Compound words, and
- Function words.

All of these activities could be incorporated into instructional practice for reading specialists and language arts teachers. Content-area teachers could focus on teaching base words, prefixes and suffixes, and compound words relevant to the new content-area vocabulary being introduced rather than as a separate activity to build morphological skills.

Use Speed Drills to Develop Automatic Recognition of Syllables and Morphemes

One way to build the automatic recognition of syllables and morphemes is through the use of quick speed drills [18]. When the quick speed drill is conducted as a challenge game to achieve a goal, it is more likely to be successful [18]. This activity would likely best be conducted by a reading specialist or a language arts instructor rather than in the context of instruction in subjectmatter and content-areas.

Teach Students the Different Syllable Types

In general, it is important to teach students the six syllable types: closed, open, vowel-consonante, vowel pair, vowel-r, and consonant-l-e. Formal instruction in these syllable types could be conducted by a reading specialist or by language arts instructors where appropriate. More generally, content-area teachers can strengthen students' literacy skills by further developing their morphological skills during activities such as content-area vocabulary instruction.

Teach the Meanings of Morphemes within the Context of a Sentence

It is important to teach morphemes across the content-area classes with attention given to the word's internal structure and meaning within the context of a sentence [43]. Instruction should include not only the spelling, but also the role the morpheme has in changing the meaning of the word. It is very common for adolescent students to make grammatical errors with the endings on words.

Inflections and derivations change the meaning of a word. Both inflections and derivations use affixes, in general mostly suffixes, to change the form of words. Inflectional affixes change such grammatical factors as tense, gender, number, or person. For instance, one could change the tense of '*jump*' from present to past tense by simply adding '*ed*' to form *jumped* or change the person of the verb '*jump*' by adding '*s*' (e.g. I *jump* versus he *jumps*).

Derivational affixes on the other hand create new words by changing the grammatical category, so for example '*jump*' the verb can be changed to a noun by adding the suffix '*er*' to form '*jumper*', the noun or by adding '*y*' to form '*jumpy*', the adjective. Derivations are the aspect of morphology that is most closely tied to achievement in reading [39].

Inflections are generally learned by the early elementary school years; however, this is not the case for derivations. Derivations are learned from the preschool years through adulthood, thus an ideal time to pursue instruction for adolescents.

What Do We Still Need to Know?

To date, little research has been done to develop instructional programs that would help children with language-learning disabilities. These students have a need to acquire strategies as well as knowledge of words, both aspects of effective morphological processing [39]. The Green et al. (2003) [43] study has documented developmental changes in the students' use of morphological forms in their writing. This study has also established preliminary connections between morphological performance in writing to include skills such as spelling and reading. However, there is a need for more research to explore the role of morphological knowledge in both the transcription as well as the text-generation stages of the writing process.

There is a need for systematic studies of methods to help adolescent students improve their awareness of morphological structure, their knowledge of affixes, and their understanding of how to untangle complex words during reading [39]. This research would provide insights into the characteristics of instructional programs that ultimately would help students with reading problems or language-learning disabilities.

Further research on the effect of morphemic structure on word reading is needed. The complex relations of sound, spelling and the meaning of morphemes in words most likely influence word reading, but these relations are not well understood [45]. Word reading in sentences or longer text versus reading words in isolation also requires more study. .

FLUENCY

Fluency is the ability to read text accurately and smoothly with little conscious attention to the mechanics of reading [6, 20, 46]. Fluent readers read text with appropriate speed, accuracy, proper intonation, and proper expression [1]. Some researchers have found a relationship between fluency and text comprehension [1, 16, 47-50], which indicates the importance of fluency. Readers must decode and comprehend to gather information from text. If the speed and accuracy of decoding words are hindered, comprehension of the words is compromised as well.

What Do Good Readers Do?

Fluent readers recognize words automatically and are better able to understand text when reading aloud or silently [1, 6]. When good readers read aloud, their reading sounds natural and expressive. Fluent readers no longer struggle with decoding words and are able to focus their attention on the meaning of the text. This allows good readers to gain a deeper knowledge of a text by making connections among the ideas presented [1]. Because fluent readers tend to be more confident about the content and meaning of what they have read, they tend to complete their work faster and with higher quality than less fluent readers [20].

What Challenges Do Adolescent Readers Face with Fluency?

Struggling readers lack fluency, read slowly, and often stop to sound out words. They may reread sections of texts to gain comprehension. Consequently, struggling adolescent readers may spend so much time and cognitive energy decoding individual words that their focus is drawn away from comprehension [1].

Another challenge facing struggling readers, and in fact all readers, is that their fluency varies based on a number of factors: the level of difficulty of the text; the degree of familiarity the reader has with the words, content, and genre of the text; and the amount of practice with the text [1]. As a result, a reader who is considered fluent at one point but does not continue to read regularly and widely could have difficulty with fluency later or in specific situations [20].

How Can Instruction Help Adolescent Students Read Fluently?

Researchers support a systematic plan of action when working to improve the fluency of struggling adolescent readers [6, 16, 20, 51, 52]. Practice is the essential component of improving fluency. The more frequently and regularly students practice reading, the more fluent they become [16, 20, 28, 51].

Remember that both decoding and vocabulary affect fluency; as a reader gains mastery over new content vocabulary; fluency is likely improved for that content area. The following suggestions for instruction promote frequent and regular practice for struggling adolescent readers.

Provide Models of Fluent Reading

Struggling readers should witness fluent reading on a regular basis. Teachers who demonstrate fluent reading during instruction give students a standard for which to strive [1, 20]. Model fluent reading for students by reading aloud from class texts frequently and regularly. Teachers should not feel that oral reading in middle and high school classes is no longer necessary.

Engage Students in Repeated Oral Reading of Texts

Research supports the use of repeated oral reading of texts to help students evelop fluency [1, 6, 16, 20, 51-53]. To establish and improve fluency, the opportunity to read aloud is preferable to silent reading opportunities, especially for struggling adolescent readers. If students are allowed only to read silently, teachers acquire little to no information about the development of fluency [1, 20, 54]. Obviously, requiring struggling readers to read aloud must be done with sensitivity so as not to embarrass students who are less fluent.

Teachers can integrate repeated reading into their instruction in the following ways:

- Provide students with frequent and regular opportunities to read passages aloud several times. Provide feedback and guidance during these oral readings.
- Allow students to practice reading aloud by themselves first to avoid the embarrassment that can occur when reading unfamiliar texts aloud. English language learners and struggling readers especially need such opportunities for practice.

Engage Students in Guided Oral Reading

Guided oral reading is a useful method of improving the fluency of struggling readers [1, 20, 27, 55]. To use guided oral reading, teachers must work individually with struggling readers on a regular basis. For middle and high school teachers, the use of guided oral reading in classes limited to an hour or less of instructional time requires that teachers target a small group of their most struggling readers and alternate working with one or two of them daily during those times when other students are engaged in group or individual work. Guided oral reading involves:

1. Asking individual students to read aloud,
2. Guiding them to self-correct when they mispronounce words, and
3. Asking questions about content to ensure comprehension.

Choral reading, or having the class read simultaneously, is not often used at the secondary level; however, if used as one of the first strategies for mastering a text, choral reading can provide struggling readers the opportunity to practice and receive support in the group before being required to read on their own [20]. Adolescents may be more accepting of choral reading if it is used with specific key passages that the teacher wants students to remember, poems, or with segments of literary works.

Engage Students in Partner Reading

Partner reading is another instructional strategy that builds fluency [1, 20]. To use partner reading:

1. Pair more fluent readers with less fluent readers;
2. Select reading partners carefully considering both compatibility and fluency;
3. Introduce the reading material by reading aloud the first paragraph or two or selected passages;
4. Inform students that partners are to select different passages to read aloud and that they should both first read each passage silently; and
5. Have partners take turns reading aloud to one another.

When fluent readers read, they provide a model for less fluent readers. As a listener, the more fluent reader can also provide feedback and support to the less fluent reader. Teachers need to provide guidance to the whole class on how to provide constructive feedback after listening to a partner read [1, 20]. This guidance may include a checklist of fluency criteria for the listener. Classroom teachers can work with the school's reading specialist, special education teacher, or reading coach to determine an appropriate list of criteria for listeners that is manageable within a content-area classroom context. Engaging students in partner reading, as opposed to asking students to read aloud for the whole class, may reduce the level of embarrassment that is felt by some struggling adolescent readers when they are asked to read aloud for the entire class.

What Do We Still Need to Know?

All of the instructional strategies suggested in this section for improving fluency recommend encouraging adolescents to read more often in the presence and with the guidance of a more fluent reader. Research has yet to reveal whether or how much improvement in reading rate is adequate to improve fluency and comprehension. The nature of the relationship between fluency and accuracy in word recognition in struggling adolescent readers also requires further study. Finally, the effects of oral versus silent fluency instruction need to be explored in greater depth [16].

VOCABULARY

Vocabulary refers to words that are used in speech and print to communicate. Vocabulary can be divided into two types: oral and print [6, 56]. Vocabulary knowledge is important to reading because the oral and written use of words promotes comprehension and communication. The three primary types of vocabulary are *oral vocabulary*, which refers to words that are recognized and used in speaking; *aural vocabulary*, which refers to the collection of words a student understands when listening to others speak; and *print vocabulary*, which refers to words used in reading and writing. Print vocabulary is more difficult to attain than oral vocabulary because it relies upon quick, accurate, and automatic recognition of the written word. Furthermore, the words, figures of speech, syntax (the grammatical arrangement of words in sentences), and text structures of printed material are more complex and obscure than that of conversational language [32]. A few studies have suggested that vocabulary instruction leads to improved comprehension [1, 6, 56, 57].

In addition to distinctions between oral, aural, and print vocabulary, vocabulary is categorized according to whether it is typically used in an informal or formal setting. Vocabulary used in a formal, educational setting is referred to as *academic vocabulary* [24, 25]. Researchers who investigate academic vocabulary knowledge typically categorize words into three areas: (1) high-frequency, everyday words (e.g., building, bus driver, eraser, etc.); (2) non-specialized academic words that occur across content areas (e.g., examine, cause, formation); and (3) specialized content-area words that are unique to specific disciplines (e.g., ecosystem, foreshadowing, octagon) [24, 25].

Two important skills that are associated with vocabulary development are *word identification* and *word analysis* [16, 57]. *Word identification* or *decoding* refers to the ability to correctly decipher a particular word out of a group of letters.

Word analysis is defined as the process involved in understanding the letters, sounds, and roots, prefixes, and suffixes that make up words, to enable a student to understand and use those words [16, 32]. Word knowledge also includes *syntactic awareness* or awareness of the grammatical use of a word, such as the part of speech represented by a word [58]. We assume that students successfully analyze a word when they articulate its meaning and use it correctly in sentences that indicate understanding of both the word's meaning and correct syntactic usage.

Once words are recognized, students use *pragmatic awareness*, or sensitivity to how words are used to communicate, to understand the purposes of their use [58]. All of these processes together constitute students' vocabulary knowledge. Word identification or recognition without comprehension of the meaning and use of a word reveals a deficiency in vocabulary knowledge.

What Skills Do Good Readers Have?

Good readers know a wide range of oral and print vocabulary. Typically, vocabulary knowledge results from extensive and repeated exposures to words through reading and speaking. One study estimated that good readers read approximately one million words per year [58]. Good readers have superior vocabulary knowledge and possess the following characteristics.

Good Readers Have Strong Oral/Aural Vocabulary

A reader's *oral vocabulary* is the collection of words used in speaking [1]. Skilled readers are able to use grade-level words fluently and clearly in their speech and understand those words when used by others in their speech. Oral/aural vocabulary ability transfers to reading once the written word has been deciphered. A skilled reader can recognize that word again with little effort [1, 16]. To do this, readers must develop their decoding skills to the point that decoding occurs effortlessly.

Good Readers Have Strong Print Vocabulary

Skilled readers are able to read words in written text at or above their grade level and use these words in written communication [1, 16]. When good readers encounter unfamiliar words, many translate this text into speech, either by decoding or getting help from someone else. Once the word is verbalized, good readers automatically recognize the word or engage in a self-regulated process to discover its meaning. This may include but is not limited to analyzing the word's morphology (roots and affixes) and syntax (part of speech), searching for context clues, or looking up the word in the dictionary [1, 16].

What Challenges Do Adolescent Readers Face with Vocabulary?

Because word identification is one of the foundational processes of reading, middle and high school students with poor or impaired word identification skills face serious challenges in their academic work. Some struggling adolescent readers have difficulty decoding and recognizing multi-syllabic words. For example, words such as "accomplishment" leave many struggling readers unsure about pronunciation or meaning. This is often the case not just because their vocabulary is limited, but also because they are unaware of or not proficient in word-learning strategies based on understanding the meanings and functions of affixes (e.g., prefixes and suffixes) and other word parts [1, 16, 20]. In content areas in which text is more technical and abstract, insufficient vocabulary knowledge can become especially problematic for struggling readers. A major goal of vocabulary instruction is to facilitate students' ability to comprehend text [1, 6, 56, 57].

In addition, the meanings of many words vary from context to context and from subject to subject, making academic vocabulary especially difficult to acquire. For example, the word meter has distinct definitions in different content areas. In literature, a meter is a poetic rhythm and in math, it is a unit of measurement. In science, a meter is a device for measuring flow. Students may experience difficulty if they do not understand that words have multiple meanings [59].

How Can Instruction Help Adolescent Students with Vocabulary?

Research findings suggest that there is not a single best way to teach vocabulary [56, 57]; rather, using a variety of techniques that include repeated exposures to unknown word meanings produces the best results. Traditionally, independent word-learning strategies, such as the use of dictionaries and context clues, have been common strategies for teaching new vocabulary. Dictionary usage involves multiple skills, such as using guidewords, decoding, and discerning correct definitions [56, 57]. Using context clues involves integrating different types of information from text to figure out unknown vocabulary. These strategies are helpful after multiple encounters with a word but should be used in combination with other instructional practices [56, 57].

The following vocabulary development strategies have been found to be effective in improving adolescent literacy levels.

Pre-Teach Difficult Vocabulary

Pre-teaching vocabulary facilitates the reading of new text by giving students the meanings of the words before they encounter them. This practice reduces the number of unfamiliar words encountered and facilitates greater vocabulary acquisition and comprehension [1]. Leaving students on their own to grasp the content material as well as to decode possibly unfamiliar vocabulary is setting them up for failure. Teachers can introduce both the more unfamiliar specialized academic words that will be used in the lesson as well as non-specialized academic words used when talking about the content.

When considering which non-specialized academic words to emphasize, teachers should consider the structure or structures used in the text. Text structures organize ideas and information according to certain patterns. For example, cause and effect patterns show the relationship between results and the events, people, or ideas that cause the results to occur. Common text structures include cause/effect, problem/solution, comparison/contrast, chronological order or sequence, concept idea with examples, proposition with support, analysis and evaluation of perspectives, arguments, and interpretations. Once the text structure or structures have been determined, teachers can identify non-specialized academic vocabulary words that help students talk about the content within a cause/effect text structure [60]. Examples of non-specialized academic words that are commonly used when talking about cause/effect texts include *recognize, analyze, result, impact,* and *relationship.*

Teachers can use the following guidelines when selecting vocabulary to pre-teach:

- Importance of the word for understanding the text;
- Students' prior knowledge of the word and the concept to which it relates;

- The existence of multiple meanings of the word (e.g., meter in poetry, mathematics, and science);
- Opportunities for grouping words together to enhance understanding a concept [56].

Once vocabulary words have been selected, teachers should consider how to make repeated exposures to the word or concept productive and enjoyable. For example, when introducing a particular word, pronounce it slowly to draw attention to each syllable, provide the word's meaning, examine word parts (e.g., prefix, root, suffix), write the word on the board, use it in a sentence, and ask a question using the word.

After introducing all words, have students work in pairs or small teams to create groups of related words and to label these groups. Students can then take turns explaining to the class their reasons for grouping words in a particular manner. Students can also work in pairs to check each other's understanding of the new words [56]. Such activities provide multiple exposures to new words and can be structured in ways that are engaging and enjoyable for students.

Use Direct, Explicit, and Systematic Instruction to Teach Difficult Vocabulary

Scientific research supports the use of direct, explicit, and systematic instruction for teaching vocabulary [1, 35]. Vocabulary lessons should be fast-paced, brief, multi-sensory, and interactive (i.e., allow students to see and write new words as well as to hear and speak these words) [16].

Explicit instruction of vocabulary involves the following steps:

1. Explain word meanings and model usage of difficult content-area vocabulary in sentences that are relevant to the subject matter concepts that students are currently learning.
2. Guide students to practice using the vocabulary in different sentences and contexts and provide corrective feedback.
3. Provide time for independent practice with the vocabulary – peer tutoring, reciprocal teaching, and collaborative learning.
4. Repeat these instructional steps until students are able to use the new vocabulary independently in their reading and writing [1, 35].

Use Students' Prior Knowledge and Provide Opportunities for Multiple Exposures to New Words

To learn and retain new words and concepts, students need to connect these words and concepts to what they already know. They also need repeated exposure to the words and concepts plus opportunities to practice using them in different contexts. Teachers can facilitate struggling readers' learning and retention of new vocabulary in the following ways:

- Prior to pre-teaching vocabulary, elicit students' prior knowledge of the content in which the new vocabulary is used and then relate their prior knowledge to the new vocabulary. It is also helpful to make a word map on the board, chart paper, or overhead to show the connections between students' prior knowledge and the new vocabulary [6].
- Provide multiple repetitions of the words in different contexts [6]. For example, within the context of explaining new concepts, giving directions, or summarizing ideas, use the new words repeatedly. You may also want to pronounce these words more slowly and pause after saying them to allow students time to identify and focus on the words.
- Point out that in academic settings certain non-specialized academic words are used when talking about content. Point out and model usage of these words and phrases. For example, when reading about or discussing the causes of the civil war, point out and model usage of such words as *cause, consequence, relationship*, etc. Guide students to use these words in their speech and writing.
- Provide students several opportunities to apply new word meanings across different situations [6]. For example, place students in small groups to discuss their understandings of the new words. Have them develop their own word maps to show relationships among the new words and connections to the important concepts. A word map is a diagram used to help show the relationships of various topics or concepts to a chosen word or phrase (See Appendix E). Have them write sentences using the new words in different ways, then share these orally with the class.

Even more repetition and time with new vocabulary should be allowed for students with learning disabilities. English language learners also require more exposure and practice with English vocabulary [56].

Use Computer Technology to Help Teach New Vocabulary

Vocabulary instruction using computer technology can be particularly helpful to struggling readers who need additional practice with vocabulary skills [1, 56]. Computer technology allows for engaging formats, such as interfaces modeled on computer games. Hyperlinks that allow students to click on words and icons can add depth to word learning. Students may find online dictionaries more useful and accessible than print dictionaries. Computers also provide access to content-area-related websites hosted by such institutions as museums and libraries. Finally, computer program animation may hold students' attention longer than plain text [59].

What Do We Still Need to Know?

Research has yet to demonstrate the most effective types of professional development needed for teachers to become proficient in vocabulary instruction. Fully equipping the teachers to address adequately the issue of vocabulary in classrooms is an important step toward improving the vocabulary of adolescents. Another gap in the knowledge base is improved understanding of how vocabulary instruction should be integrated with comprehension instruction. We know that repetition and prior knowledge help familiarize adolescents with new vocabulary, but we need to determine what instructional techniques can help educators ensure that adolescents grasp the contextual meanings of vocabulary [1, 11, 61].

TEXT COMPREHENSION

Comprehension is the process of *extracting or constructing meaning* (building new meanings and integrating new with old information) from words once they have been identified [58]. Many struggling adolescent readers do not have difficulty reading words accurately; they have difficulty making sense of the information and ideas conveyed by the text [6, 62]. Comprehension varies depending on the text being read. Even proficient readers may have difficulty comprehending particular texts from time to time. Difficulties with comprehension may result from a reader's unfamiliarity with the content, style, or syntactic structures of the text [58, 63]. Even as adults, many people struggle when reading Shakespeare or the manual for installing a new computer program.

What Do Good Readers Do?

Good adolescent readers are purposeful, strategic, and critical readers who understand the content presented in various types of texts.

Good Readers Set a Purpose For Reading

Successful readers establish different purposes for reading different kinds of text. They read computer manuals to figure out how to use a new computer or software program. They read the newspaper to find out what is happening in the community. They read mystery novels for enjoyment. Good readers know that there are many purposes for reading, and they vary the ways in which they read depending on their purposes and the texts [58, 63].

Good Readers are Strategic Readers

Successful readers are mentally active readers. They make sense of what they read by drawing on knowledge and experiences that are relevant to the information and ideas in the text. Good readers use knowledge of vocabulary, language structures, and genre to understand the text. They have a repertoire of reading strategies that is used before, during, and after reading to build meaning from the text [7, 58]. For example, before beginning a new mystery novel, good readers may consider the author; the book's tone, organization, literary elements; and other books written by the author.

While reading a mystery novel, for example, successful readers constantly try to predict what will happen next. They also make text-to-text connections; that is, they use information from previous mysteries that they have read to help understand the new mystery. Good readers monitor their comprehension while reading by periodically checking their level of understanding of the text. If problems occur with comprehension while reading, good readers possess knowledge of useful "fix-up" strategies and implement them to gain a better understanding of what is being read [7, 58].

Successful adolescent readers use post-reading strategies, such as summarizing, to help remember what they have read and to clarify misunderstandings. When good readers read a chapter in a history text, they know that, at the end of each section, it is helpful to stop and summarize what has been learned so as to better understand and retain new information. Good readers also know and are able to apply a variety of reading strategies to help them comprehend what they read [7, 58].

Good Readers are Critical Readers

Comprehension is necessary but not sufficient for developing adolescents' critical awareness of all texts [63]. Critical readers analyze how writers, illustrators, and others involved represent people and their ideas. To be fully literate, adolescents must develop a critical awareness of how all texts position them as readers and must consider such factors as how authors' backgrounds and cultures influence their writing [63-65]. Good readers apply critical thinking skills to texts found in printed and electronic media to consider how authors manipulate electronic and print information in different ways and for varying purposes [63].

What Challenges Do Adolescent Readers Face with Text Comprehension?

Adolescents struggle with text comprehension for different reasons. Some adolescents simply lack sufficient fluency to achieve comprehension. Some fluent students lack comprehension strategies, such as generating questions, summarizing, and clarifying misunderstandings. Others have learned strategies only in the context of reading narrative texts, such as stories. Some students learn on their own how to transfer strategies used in one domain, such as literature, to other domains, such as history and science. Other students do not learn how to transfer these strategies on their own and are never taught how to apply them to the expository text found in science, history, math, and other content areas. Still other students have limited background knowledge in these domains [46, 66].

The structure of middle and high school texts also presents challenges for struggling readers. Expository text is the most prevalent text structure in most middle and high school texts. In contrast with narrative text, students have had less exposure to expository text and, more important, have not been taught comprehension strategies within the context of expository text [60]. Common categories of expository text are cause/effect, problem/solution, comparison/contrast, chronological order or sequence, concept idea with examples, and proposition with support. Students encounter expository text across their content-area courses. Expository text is found in newspaper and magazine articles, science and social studies texts, research articles, and primary source documents. The prevalence of expository text categories varies by discipline. For example, chronological order and cause/effect are common in history texts. Geography texts make frequent use of description and comparison/contrast. Social studies texts use analysis and evaluation of perspectives, arguments, and interpretations using proposition-support structures [60]. If students are not familiar with the various types of texts used in middle and high school, they may encounter challenges in comprehending what they read.

How Can Instruction Help Adolescent Students with Text Comprehension?

Although many struggling adolescent readers need more specific and intense instruction in reading from reading specialists, all teachers can assume responsibility for helping students comprehend texts that are used in their classrooms. The goal of text comprehension instruction is to help students become active, purposeful, and independent readers of science, history, literary, and mathematics texts. Key findings from research show that learning how to use comprehension strategies can improve adolescent readers' text comprehension [1, 35, 46, 62]. The following sections describe the comprehension strategies teachers can incorporate into their content-area instruction and suggestions for teaching these strategies so that students can use them independently.

Integrate Text Comprehension Strategies into Instruction
Some comprehension strategies are general and can be used across different kinds of text. The following strategies can be adapted for use with most types of text [67].
Generate Questions. Good readers ask questions before, during, and after reading. Generating questions is a way to process text and monitor comprehension. Asking questions during reading helps students monitor their understanding of what they have read and integrate different parts of the text to understand main ideas and important concepts. Teachers can integrate instruction in generating questions into their lessons using the following steps:

1. Read aloud passages from subject-matter text;
2. As you read, stop now and then to model the kinds of questions successful readers ask themselves as they read. For example, "Why does the author tell me this?" "Did I understand this correctly?" "What seems to be the most important point or idea?";
3. Repeat this modeling several times with different texts; and

4. Guide students in generating their own questions with content-area texts [1, 35, 36].

Answer Questions. Teacher questioning is an effective way to help students think about what they have read so that they can more fully comprehend the text. Teachers can use *question-answering instruction* to help students improve how they answer questions, which will, in turn, help them better understand what they read. In question-answering instruction, teachers must create opportunities for question answering and must also help students to determine the kind of response called for by the question. The teacher must then model how to construct various responses. Using content-area texts, teachers can model how to construct answers from:

- Explicit information in the text, that is, the answer is evident in the text and can often can be copied or repeated (sometimes referred to as a "right there" response);
- Implicit information found in several different places in the text; that is, the answer is in the text, but the reader has to pull it together from different parts of the text (sometimes referred to as a "pulling it together" response);
- Implicit information found in the text and the reader's own prior knowledge and experiences, that is, the answer must be generated from a synthesis of information from the text and the reader's prior knowledge and experiences (sometimes referred to as a "text and me" response); and
- Students' prior knowledge and experiences alone; that is, the student does not have to read the text to answer the question, but reading the text will inform the answer (sometimes referred to as an "on my own" response) [1, 35, 36].

Below is a sample text with corresponding questions that elicit the four types of responses described above.

Margie went into the schoolroom. It was right next to her bedroom, and the mechanical teacher was on, waiting for her. It was always on at the same time everyday except Saturday and Sunday because her mother said little girls learned better if they learned at regular hours.

The screen was lit up, and it said, "Today's arithmetic lesson is on the addition of proper fractions. Please insert yesterday's homework in the proper slot."
Margie put her homework in the slot with a sigh. She was thinking about the old schools they had when her grandfather's grandfather was a little boy. All the kids from the whole neighborhood came laughing and shouting into the schoolyard, sitting together in the same schoolroom, going home together at the end of the day. They learned the same things, so they could help one another on the homework and talk about it. And the teachers were people... The mechanical teacher flashed on the screen: "When we add the fractions 1/2 and 1/4..." Margie was thinking about how the kids must have loved it in the old days. She was thinking about the fun they had.

a.   *Excerpted from The Fun They Had by Isaac Asimov [68]*
b.   *Who was the author of this story? ("Right there" question)*
c.   *What does Margie like about the "old schools"? ("Pulling it together" question)*
d.   *When does this story take place? ("Text and me" question)*
e.   *Should we have "mechanical" teachers? ("On my own" question)*

Monitor Comprehension. Expert readers monitor their comprehension as they read by continuously identifying when they do and when they do not comprehend the information, ideas, and other messages contained in the text. When comprehension breaks down, expert readers are able to use comprehension monitoring or other problem solving strategies to help them comprehend. Many struggling readers do not use monitoring strategies or use them inappropriately [1, 35, 36].

Because comprehension monitoring is a mental process that cannot be observed, teachers must find ways to replicate or model this process for struggling readers. Teachers can make apparent to students the monitoring strategies they themselves use when reading by verbalizing these strategies as they read a text passage. To model the use of monitoring strategies, use the following steps:

1.   Read aloud selected text passages.
2.   Stop at various points to "think aloud" about what may or may not be understood. An example of how questioning, prediction, and summarizing are used as monitoring strategies is given in the box below. Also see Appendix A for additional examples.

3. Provide examples of other problem-solving strategies and how they are used in response to comprehension difficulties. Examples of problem-solving strategies include re-reading the text, asking oneself questions about the text, and reading before or after the portion of text where comprehension difficulties occurred [1, 35, 36]. Again, see Appendix A for examples.

The teacher reads aloud the title of a newspaper article. "'Do or Die Time for the Kiwi.' I'm confused. I thought kiwi was a kind of fruit. How can a kiwi fruit have 'do or die time'? Maybe farmers are having problems growing kiwi fruit...? I need to read more to find out if I'm right." The teacher reads aloud the next sentence from the article. "'Although they're 0-4, the Kiwi Curlers may still have winnable games against Germany and Italy.' Oh I get it, curling must be some kind of sport because it talks about "winnable games" and a score of 0-4. I don't really know anything about curling, but I do know that this article is about sports and Kiwi is the name of one of the teams. The article must have something to do with the Olympics because I know the Olympics are going on now and it says that the Kiwi team is playing against other countries—Germany and Italy."

Summarize Text. Summarizing helps students focus on the important content of a text, determine what is important and what is not important, condense the important content, and restate this content in their own words. Summarizing helps students comprehend and remember what they read. There are four components of the summarizing strategy:

1. Identify and/or formulate main ideas,
2. Connect the main ideas,
3. Identify and delete redundancies, and
4. Restate the main ideas and connections using different words and phrasings.

Use text structure. As adolescents build their knowledge of science, social studies, mathematics, and literature, learning to use knowledge of the structure of the particular text helps them comprehend the more complex texts that they encounter in these disciplines [50, 69]. Selecting strategies that are useful for comprehending text structures involves examining the content, language, and structure of text with which students may have difficulty and then identifying specific strategies that will help students use these patterns and structures to aid in comprehension [50, 69].

Teaching students to use graphic and semantic organizers that differ based on the category of expository text the organizer represents is one way to help students understand and use text structure to comprehend complex texts. A graphic organizer that lends itself to chronological order differs from an organizer that is useful for cause and effect. Teachers can model the use of graphic organizers to show the different categories of expository text and then encourage students to use the various organizers to record and organize important information and concepts from the texts they are reading [6, 60]. Appendix B provides examples of graphic organizers that exemplify different text structures.

In additional, teachers can identify words that function as signal or transition words for a particular text structure. For example, common signal and transition words for cause/effect structures include *because, since, consequently.* Teachers can emphasize and teach the functions of these words by:

- Placing text passages on the overhead projector,
- Reading the passages aloud,
- Underlining key signal or transition words, and
- Explaining how these words provide clues for using text structure to aid comprehension.

For example, explain that when students encounter the word *consequently*, it serves as a signal for the direction that the text will take next, in this case that a result of some action or event is about to be described or discussed. Teachers can model and emphasize the use of signal or transition words orally as they discuss content and ask questions that require students to use these words in their responses [50, 69].

Use Graphic and Semantic Organizers. Teach students how to use graphic and semantic organizers to help them organize ideas and concepts during and after reading. Graphic organizers are diagrams or other visuals that help students identify and see the relationships among concepts, ideas, and facts in a text [6]. These organizers can be used with either narrative or expository text and in fact can be used to illustrate or represent the text structure itself. A semantic organizer, sometimes called a semantic map or web, is a type of graphic organizer that uses lines to connect a central concept or main idea with related or supporting facts or ideas (see Appendix B) [1, 7, 35, 36, 70].

Teaching students to use graphic and semantic organizers that differ depending on the category of expository text is one way to help students understand and use text structure to comprehend complex texts. A graphic organizer that lends itself to chronological order differs from an organizer that is useful for cause and effect. Teachers can model the use of graphic organizers to show the different categories of expository text and then encourage students to use the various organizers to record and organize important information and concepts from their texts [6, 60]. Appendix B provides examples of graphic organizers that exemplify different text structures.

Develop Critical Analysis and Reasoning Skills

To be fully literate students must be able to analyze critically the ideas and information they obtain from texts [65]. The use of graphic organizers can contribute to the development of critical analysis and reasoning skills [65].

"Inquiry" or "I" charts are a type of graphic organizer that students can use to compile, compare, and analyze information on a historical event or topic from several text sources. Procedures to guide the use of these charts are listed below:

1. Plan a topic and set of questions that can be answered in multiple texts. For example, a set of questions could be developed around the effect of the westward expansion of European Americans on the Native Americans of the Great Plains.
2. Identify several resources that address this issue from different perspectives.
3. Construct a chart or graphic organizer that has one column for each question, a row for students' prior knowledge relevant to the questions, additional rows equal to the number of sources used, and a final row for pulling together key ideas from prior knowledge and the various sources. Appendix B provides an example of an "I" chart.
4. Probe students to use their prior knowledge to answer the questions before reading the various text sources. Summaries of students' responses based on their prior knowledge are recorded in the first row.
5. Help students during reading to attend to sections of each text that respond to the questions, to summarize this information, and to record it in the chart.

6. Help students to examine the summaries of each text across the various rows to determine similarities and differences in how the texts address each of the central questions.
7. Help students pull together the ideas from the different sources (i.e., their prior knowledge and the information found in the various texts) and resolve competing ideas from the separate sources.

Strategies such as the use of "I" charts help students understand how to integrate information by attending to the connections, biases, and contexts across different texts [65].

Use Direct, Explicit, and Systematic Instruction to Teach Students to Use Text Comprehension Strategies

Scientific research supports teaching students comprehension strategies using direct, explicit, and systematic instruction. Comprehension strategy instruction is organized into three phases: (1) explicit training and teacher modeling, (2) guided practice, and (3) independent practice [1, 7, 35, 36, 70].

Phase 1: Explicit Training and Teacher Modeling. Effective strategy instruction begins with teacher talk, which can take the form of a discussion or a lecture. Whether discussion or lecture is used, instruction typically involves teaching six components:

1. The name of the strategy,
2. How to use the strategy,
3. Explicit modeling of the strategy,
4. Examples of when to use the strategy,
5. Possible adjustments to the strategy for different tasks, and
6. The usefulness of the strategy [35, 70].

Explicit modeling should be performed only after giving a thorough explanation of the strategy. The purpose of teacher modeling is to demonstrate the mental processes used by expert readers. Teachers can do this by pausing and "thinking aloud" as they read. Students observe as teachers verbalize their decision-making about which strategies to use and how they use them [35, 70].

Phase 2: Guided Practice. During this phase, students practice the strategies that they learn with support from the teacher and other students. As the guided practice phase proceeds, the teacher assumes a less active role in student strategy use. Teachers can support strategy use during this phase by:

- Breaking the strategy into simplified steps,
- Giving cue cards or checklists for strategy steps,
- Reverting to explicit instruction and modeling as necessary, and
- Allowing students to work in small groups to practice a strategy together.

Supporting students in collaborative work to learn new strategies is a critical part of guided practice [35].

Phase 3: Independent Practice and Debriefing. Teachers can incorporate independent practice into instruction by providing opportunities for students to use strategies on their own. These opportunities may include reading assignments as homework or in-class individual reading. Debriefing after independent practice is important. During debriefing, teachers ask about the strategies students used while doing their independent reading assignments, how they used those strategies, and how well the strategies worked for them [35]. A sample lesson plan for explicit comprehension strategy instruction is provided in Appendix C.

Teach Students to Use Multiple Strategies

Good readers use strategies in clusters. For example, during reading, good readers question and clarify misunderstandings; and after reading, they summarize and predict what will happen in the next part of the text. Students need to learn and practice individual strategies, but they also need to learn how to use clusters of strategies to aid comprehension [1, 35, 36]. As with individual strategy instruction, use direct, explicit, systematic instruction to teach clusters of strategies that work together. Appendix D provides information about and directions for using Reciprocal Teaching, an instructional tool that provides instruction on four different learning strategies: questioning, clarifying, summarizing, and predicting. Instructional strategy packets such as Reciprocal Teaching encourage students to move toward higher levels of thinking and comprehension by utilizing clusters of strategies [71-74].

What Do We Still Need to Know?

To increase understanding of how best to develop adolescent readers' text comprehension, research should focus on investigating the effectiveness of interventions for improving comprehension of specific kinds of text (e.g., expository text using cause and effect structures). For example, although there is evidence of the importance of having sufficient prior knowledge of the domain or topic of an academic text, it is not yet clear how best to instruct students to access this prior knowledge. Research on whether certain interventions are more or less effective with specific populations of adolescent students (e.g., English language learners with limited native language literacy) is also needed. Finally, explorations of the kinds of supplemental materials useful in enhancing content-area instruction in text comprehension would provide teachers with guidance in selecting such materials [6, 46].

SUPPORTING LITERACY DEVELOPMENT THROUGH ASSESSMENT, WRITING, AND MOTIVATIONAL STRATEGIES

As many secondary teachers have found, improving the literacy levels of students encompasses much more than simply addressing key literacy components. Researchers agree that other factors relate strongly to the degree to which adolescents are able to decode and comprehend what they read fluently [66, 75, 76].

This section focuses on some of the related components of literacy instruction at the secondary level. These components include reading assessment, writing, and motivation. The reading assessment portion of this section is organized into summative assessment, formative assessment and diagnostic assessment. As in the previous section, the writing and motivation portions of this section describe the component, explain how successful readers approach it, present the challenges adolescents face, suggest instructional techniques for addressing strategies in the classroom, and provide examples of research areas that still need to be explored.

READING ASSESSMENT

Effective instruction depends on sound instructional decision-making, which, in turn, depends on reliable data regarding students' strengths, weaknesses, and progress in learning content and developing literacy [77]. Adolescent reading difficulties may involve one or more of the literacy components described in previous sections. Without assessments that are sensitive to the contributions of each component to overall reading ability, teachers will not be able to target their instruction to the skills and strategies most in need of improvement.

This section briefly describes summative assessments and then explores three types of formative assessment that content-area teachers can integrate into instruction: teacher questioning, observation, and performance assessment. The last section describes diagnostic reading assessment. Diagnostic assessment is particularly important for struggling readers because it provides teachers with an understanding of the specific skills and strategies these readers can and cannot use [78-80]. With this information, teachers can plan literacy activities and interventions that will build on students' strengths and address their weaknesses.

Summative Assessments

Most reading assessments taken by adolescents are summative and include quizzes, end-ofchapter tests, district and statewide tests, and standardized measures of reading [77]. These assessments provide important information about adolescents' reading and subject-area achievements. Summative assessments inform teachers whether classroom-level instruction has had the desired impact. Finally, assessments provide necessary school-, district-, and state-level data, but they do not inform daily instructional decision-making, nor do they provide information on individual student progress.

Although summative assessments provide important data needed to assess the overall academic achievements of students in a class, school, district, or state, both formative and diagnostic assessments provide data that can help classroom teachers make more informed decisions about which readers can successfully undertake which activities with which texts [46].

Formative Assessments

In order to adapt instruction to students' literacy learning needs, teachers must be able to understand and track students' literacy development. Teachers use a variety of approaches to find out what they need to know about student progress in literacy development, including teacher observation, classroom discussion and the reading of students' work. These and other assessment practices become *formative assessment* when evidence from them is used to adapt instruction to meet student needs [81]. This section will address several formative assessment approaches: teacher questioning, teacher observation of students' reading strategies, and performance assessment.

Teacher Questioning

The most common form of formative assessment is teacher questioning. Typically teachers use questioning to check student comprehension after students have read a passage or chapter [77]. Teachers may conduct this questioning orally or in writing, as occurs when students are asked to complete the questions at the end of the chapter and turn them in the next day. Comprehension checks may help the teacher informally assess what students have understood; however, these checks do little to help teachers understand the reading skills and strategies students use to help them understand assigned reading. It is sometimes difficult to formulate questions that tap only the content of what was to be read; many times questions can be correctly answered without actually reading the text. Therefore, teachers should not rely solely on questioning to assess comprehension.

To assess adolescent reading, teachers can expand questioning beyond mere comprehension checks. To do so, teachers should consider teacher questioning as falling into three broad categories:

- Questions that focus on student learning of content,
- Questions that focus on the development and use of reading skills and strategies, and
- Questions that model the kinds of questions students should learn to ask themselves while reading [77].

The first category of teacher questioning allows teachers to assess how students are progressing in relation to standards and instructional goals. Whereas comprehension checks tend to be .narrowly focused on comprehension of a particular text or lecture, questions that focus on assessing student progress toward achieving standards and goals give teachers information on whether students are integrating what they have learned from reading texts, classroom discussions, teacher lectures, and other learning experiences relevant to achieving standards and goals. This first category of questioning is not directly related to assessing student reading ability; however it can provide insight into whether students are learning content through their reading.

The second category of questioning focuses on assessing the strategies and skills students are using or not using when reading. Examples of this category of questioning include: "Can you tell me how you figured out the meaning of *exotic*?" and, "What are some strategies you can use to find out what this chapter is about?" Teachers can use this type of questioning regularly and in a systematic manner by keeping a daily record of the kinds of questions asked, with which students, and whether responses were appropriate.

The last category of teacher questioning involves both instruction and assessment. By modeling strategic questioning for their students, teachers are instructing students on the kinds of questions they should be asking themselves while reading. Teachers can then assess students' use of these types of questions by teaching them to keep a record of the questions they ask themselves when reading. Frequent review of this information informs teachers of whether individual students are making progress in monitoring comprehension using self-questioning. This information can then be used to inform subsequent instruction in reading strategies and skills.

Teacher Observation of Students' Reading Strategies

The use of student "think alouds" is one way that teachers can observe the reading strategies students use while reading. When students think aloud as they read, they describe the strategies that they use to make sense of a text. This practice allows the teacher to uncover the details of students' reading strengths and weaknesses within the context of content-area reading. Thinking aloud must be explicitly modeled and explained by the teacher prior to asking students to use it. Appendix A includes instructions on how to model strategy use through thinking aloud. Once students have seen teachers modeling strategies through the think aloud process, they can begin to practice thinking aloud with a partner and then by themselves. As with teacher questioning, keeping a record of the reading strategies students report using in their think alouds and reviewing this information regularly inform the teacher of whether individual students are making progress in using particular strategies when reading. Moreover, this assessment information provides direction to teachers on the reading strategies they need to emphasize with students in their instruction [77].

Performance Assessment

Performance assessments require students to demonstrate the ability to use what they have learned from content texts. Most performance assessments simulate tasks or aspects of tasks that are deemed important to higher education, the workplace, and civic life. Performance assessments typically use prompts that are constructed so that student responses result in complex tasks [77]. For example, a performance assessment prompt might direct students to read two articles that provide differing accounts of an historical event and provide a rationale for the different accounts and conclusions reached in the articles.

Performance assessments in content-area classrooms provide insight into students' abilities to use what they have learned from their subject-area reading [77, 82]. Rubrics and examples of performance are important components of performance assessment. Rubrics provide details about different levels of performance. Teachers can share rubrics with their students to help them understand expectations for performance and how the assessment will be graded. Examples of student work are another helpful source of information on the types of performances considered standard or above standard. Teacher discussion of rubrics and student work samples gives students clear guidance on the components that must be evident in their work. Teachers can also use rubrics and student work samples to instruct students in how to achieve standard or superior performance.

Ongoing and reflective use of performance assessments in concert with rubrics, performance levels, and student work samples can help students understand and gain control over their own assessment efforts [77, 82].

Although useful, performance assessments present several challenges. Most performance assessments assume that students have understood the reading that they are asked to apply in the assessment. These assessments do not help teachers understand students' reading skills and strategies. Students' writing skills may influence their ability to succeed in an assessment that requires written responses. Personal characteristics of a student, such as confidence and selfesteem, influence performance on assessments requiring oral responses. Finally, student performance is difficult to score reliably. Consistent scoring requires teacher expertise, substantial scoring training, and time [77, 82].

Using teacher questioning, teacher observation, and performance tasks to assess classroom reading assumes that content-area teachers understand reading assessment, yet few teacher preparation programs or professional development sessions attend to classroom-based reading assessment in the content areas, particularly at the secondary level. Content-area teachers need professional development in formative reading assessment that involves teacher questioning; observation; performance assessment; the use of records, checklists, and other means of recording students' strengths, weaknesses, and progress; and how to use this information in their instruction. Moreover, the content-area curriculum must be altered to allow time for teachers to observe students as readers of content-area texts [77].

Diagnostic Assessments

Diagnostic assessments provide teachers with a more precise understanding of individual students' strengths and weaknesses [78-80]. Diagnosis involves measuring, assessing, and evaluating a student's reading abilities and then identifying appropriate content and learning activities that will facilitate the student's reading development. Diagnostic assessment is typically administered, scored, and interpreted by a reading specialist, special education teacher, or school psychologist [78-80].

The ability to diagnose reading difficulties begins with high quality assessment instruments that are reliable, valid, and have the sensitivity and precision to identify individual students' strengths and weaknesses in a manner that is useful for planning instruction [78-80]. Currently few such instruments exist for diagnosing adolescents' reading ability [46, 58].

For younger readers, diagnostic assessments are typically performed by a reading specialist or special education teacher, who then shares results and instructional implications with gradelevel teachers. Despite the lack of effective diagnostic reading assessments for older students, the classroom teacher, in collaboration with a specialist trained in conducting diagnostic assessment, can use the process of diagnostic assessment to determine the strengths and weaknesses of struggling readers [78, 79, 82]. In general, this process requires the specialist and teacher to work together to (1) assess a student's reading performance, strategies, and skills; (2) evaluate the student's performance, strategies, and skills in relation to academic expectations; (3) evaluate texts in relation to the student's literacy and content learning needs; (4) assess and evaluate the student's ability to learn and the optimal conditions for that learning to occur; and (5) design instruction that integrates information learned in steps one through four and that results in content and literacy development [76].

Collaboration with the reading specialist or special education teacher enables teachers to create a profile of students' reading strengths and difficulties. Questions such as the following may be used to guide this diagnostic process [78]:

- What is the student's current level of overall reading ability? Is this level satisfactory for comprehending the texts used in content-area classrooms?
- Which reading strategies and skills are strengths for the student? Which reading strategies and skills are limitations for the student? For example, does the student have sufficient mastery of decoding and fluency so that instruction can concentrate on comprehension?
- What other factors (e.g., a learning disability, vision or hearing problems) might be associated with the student's reading ability?
- What are the best instructional conditions for the student? For example, whereas some students learn best when working with their peers; other students learn best alone. English language learners often need additional support and time to develop the vocabulary and language structures associated with particular academic domains and texts.
- What are some recommendations for the student's reading instruction, both in the content-area classroom and in the reading classroom?

Evidence that addresses these questions should be derived from multiple sources [46, 82]. Examples of possible sources include diagnostic assessments used by the reading specialist or other professional assessing the student, teacher questioning and observation, performance assessment, a student read-aloud of a passage, a student think-aloud, and evidence of the development of reading proficiency in the various subcomponents of reading.

Teachers and reading specialists or special education teachers can implement these recommendations by using student profiles, continuing to assess as they teach, reconvening to determine whether the instruction was effective, and determining next steps [82].

What Do We Still Need to Know?

Studies are needed to establish reliable and valid measurement strategies and instruments to develop well-defined, evidence-based treatment interventions for all of the literacy-related components mentioned in this text. This text emphasizes strategy instruction because it has been found to be effective in helping adolescents read better. Yet a debate continues about whether or not the effectiveness of strategy instruction should be assessed by reading achievement or subject matter achievement [1, 79, 80]. These are important questions that need to be answered to move closer to accurate assessment of adolescent reading.

WRITING

Writing is the ability to compose text effectively for various purposes and audiences [83]. Writing is a tool for communication and learning that allows us to document, collect, and widely circulate detailed information [75]. Writing also provides a means of expressing oneself and persuading others. Writing, however, is not just a method of communication and expression. Several researchers have found that, much like reading, improving one's writing skills improves one's capacity to learn [4, 61, 84, 85], and learning to write well requires instruction. In addition, many of the skills that are involved in writing, such as grammar and spelling, reinforce and are reinforced by reading skills [66]. Therefore, teachers who can contribute to improving the writing of struggling adolescent readers should positively affect these students' literacy levels.

What Do Good Writers Do?

As the demands of content instruction increase, so do literacy demands in both reading and writing. Students are expected to read and write across various genres and disciplines [58, 75, 86]. Skilled writers employ different types of strategies to help navigate the writing process. Skilled writers learn to be self-directed and goal-oriented. Good writers employ self-regulation strategies that help them to plan, organize, and revise their own work independently [33, 75, 83]. Self-regulation strategies include goal setting, self-instruction, and self-monitoring. Good writers are aware of and able to compose various text genres [33, 75, 83], such as narrative, persuasive, and descriptive essays.

What Challenges Do Adolescent Readers Face with Writing?

Students who do not write well are at a disadvantage because they lack an effective communication and learning tool. Furthermore, the inability to write well greatly limits adolescents' opportunities for education and future employment [33, 75, 87]. Finally, teachers use writing to assess the content knowledge of students, so those students who do not write well often suffer academically [33, 75, 83].

How Can Instruction Help Adolescent Students with Writing?

Several instructional strategies have been found to be effective in improving the writing of struggling adolescent readers. These strategies include using direct, explicit, and systematic instruction; teaching students the importance of prewriting; providing a supportive instructional environment; using rubrics to assess writing; and addressing the diverse needs of individual students.

Use Direct, Explicit, and Systematic Instruction to Teach Writing

Direct, explicit, and systematic instruction is the most widely suggested instructional practice for improving writing skills. Directly teaching adolescent writers strategies and skills that enhance writing development allows educators to build upon students' prior knowledge and introduce new information contextually [33, 75, 83]. Examples of strategies and skills that can be taught across content areas include the steps of the writing process (planning, drafting, revising, and editing) and skills relevant to editing and revision (See Appendixes F and G). To use direct, explicit, and systematic instruction in writing:

1. Explain the writing skill or strategy and model how to apply it in writing in a manner that is similar to what students will be asked to do,
2. Guide students in using the skills and strategies in their writing assignments and provide corrective feedback,
3. Provide time and opportunities for independent practice with the writing skills and strategies, and
4. Repeat these instructional steps until students are able to use them independently in their writing.

Teach Students the Importance of Prewriting

Students need to learn the steps of the writing process (planning, drafting, revising, and editing) [75, 86]. Too often students do not take the time to plan before they write nor do they revise and edit after they write. Research has indicated that prewriting or planning, in particular, provides students with time to figure out what they know about their topic and organize their thoughts [88, 89]. Regardless of the content area, prewriting or planning is helpful.

In a typical ninth grade social studies class, students might be expected to write an essay or a research report on the industrialization of America. Prewriting allows students to think through what they know about American industrialization and what they might need to research regarding this topic. In addition, the organization of the essay or report can be planned during this prewriting stage.

The most common types of prewriting strategies taught are:

1. Brainstorming and making lists,
2. Developing outlines, and
3. Using graphic organizers [75, 88].

These planning activities can help students shape their loosely organized thoughts and ideas into a useful framework [88]. With brainstorming, teachers should encourage students to speak and think freely. It is only later that the most relevant information to the topic is extracted from the list created from the brainstorming activity. Outlines have the potential to become too elaborate for struggling adolescent readers, so teachers should encourage students to prepare less detailed outlines to help frame their thoughts [88]. These outlines could be only three layers with main topics, subtopics, and supporting details Graphic organizers, such as spider maps, series-of-events chains, and compare-and-contrast matrices, are useful in helping students to visualize connections between the information to be included in an essay or report (see Appendix B) [6, 88, 90].

Provide a Supportive Instructional Environment for Students
Writing skills are best developed with practice in a supportive instructional environment [83]. Providing students with substantial support at each step of the writing process is important to their success with writing [33, 75, 83]. Suggestions for providing a supportive environment for writing include:

• Make writing a regular part of the activities in every class, across content areas;
• Give students opportunities to engage in extended writing;
• Ask leading questions that prompt students to plan next steps in the writing process. For example, you might ask a student who has decided to write about cars but has not decided what type of writing to

produce, "So would you like to create your own story about cars or persuade someone that one kind of car is better than another?";

- Model a love for writing by sharing your work with students;
- Convey the ways in which writing will be useful to them in their lives outside of school;
- Connect writing to reading and other academic subjects; and
- Display the students' writings in prominent places.

Using Rubrics to Assess Writing

Although this section describes writing instructional strategies that may be useful to teachers as they teach within their content area, it is important to address how the writing will be assessed. Assessment tools such as rubrics are available, and teachers should make students aware of these tools during instruction so that the students will understand the standards and expectations of good writing before they begin the writing process. In addition, students can use the rubrics to evaluate their own writing and the writing of their peers. Thus, the rubric becomes an assessment tool for the educator while also promoting self-evaluation, student autonomy, and student collaboration [91]. Rubrics are important in assessing writing because they do not simply attribute a grade or score to the writing assignment but detail a clearer understanding of strong and weak areas. This insight provides students the information needed to improve their writing [83].

Address the Needs of Diverse Learners

A "one-size-fits-all" writing program does not address the diverse needs that are encountered by most teachers in their classrooms. The needs of struggling adolescent writers vary depending upon their prior knowledge, skills, motivation, and level of self-regulation. Periodically allowing students to write about a topic of their choice is an important means of promoting individual diversity and tapping into the personal interests of students. Teachers should strive to motivate struggling adolescents to write by exploring topics of interest to them [33, 75, 83]. Teachers need to stress the importance, particularly in high school instruction, of the significance and usefulness of writing beyond the classroom and emphasize the value of writing in success in college or in the workplace.

What Do We Still Need to Know?

Although a review of existing literature provides insight into how to teach writing to adolescents, research is needed to understand how best to identify, prevent, and remediate writing difficulties. Research is needed to explore the role of the key literacy components (phonemic awareness, phonics, vocabulary, fluency, and comprehension) in the development of adolescents' writing ability. Finally, additional research is needed to investigate how adolescents' beliefs about their writing ability impact the development of their reading ability [33, 75, 76]. This type of research is important to promote a better understanding of the relationship between reading and writing development in adolescents and to design more effective instructional approaches to support overall literacy development in adolescents.

MOTIVATION

An individual's goals, values, and beliefs regarding the topics, processes, and outcomes of reading affect students' motivations for reading [34, 92]. This implies that (1) readers are in control of their motivation, and (2) they have goals they are striving to reach by using reading or writing tasks [34, 92-94]. Motivation also involves self-efficacy, or the belief that one is capable of success. Previous successful performance in reading is critical to adolescents' positive sense of self-efficacy in reading and motivation to continue reading [82, 92, 94]. Finally, motivation for reading, along with background knowledge, appropriate reading strategies, and interaction with others, contributes to reading engagement. Engaged readers tend to enjoy reading and to read more frequently; reading frequency, in turn, is related to a number of positive outcomes, including reading achievement [92, 93].

What Do Motivated Readers Do?

Motivated readers and writers share several attributes that support motivation. These attributes include self-determination, self-regulation, and engagement [34, 92, 93].

Self-Determination

Motivated readers and writers are self-determined; that is, they perceive that they have control over their reading and writing tasks. Even when assignments are highly structured and teacherdriven, motivated readers and writers understand that they have choices regarding how to complete the assignment [92, 93, 95, 96].

Self-Regulation

Motivated readers and writers self-regulate; they direct their reading and writing performance toward goals that they want to achieve [92, 93, 95, 97]. Self-regulation involves understanding the subtasks of a reading or writing activity and employing strategies that aid in completing these subtasks. For example, if the assignment is to write an essay that compares and contrasts two characters from a novel, motivated writers ensure that they understand the teacher's expectations for the assignment. Motivated writers also employ such strategies as taking notes on the two characters while reading, using a diagram to organize notes for the essay, and making an outline before writing the essay [92].

Engagement

Motivation can lead to engagement, and engagement can lead to increased motivation. However, a motivated reader or writer does not necessarily become an engaged reader or writer. Some readers and writers may lose their motivation due to poor skills or insufficient background knowledge of the topic [77]. Engagement involves the interdependent operation of motivation, prior knowledge, and effective and efficient strategy use in a literacy activity, such as reading a story or writing an essay [86, 96].

Engaged readers and writers are always motivated, and once they are engaged in a specific reading or writing task, take pleasure in it and are motivated to continue with the task because of the pleasure it brings. Furthermore, the engagement experienced in accomplishing one task increases motivation for future tasks of a similar nature [92, 93, 98].

What Challenges Do Adolescent Readers Face with Motivation?

A number of factors influence adolescents' declines in motivation. As students enter adolescence, most experience changes in their beliefs, values, and goals that can lead to a decline in motivation [34, 93, 99]. Adolescents may lack motivation in school, but outside of school they may read magazines of personal interest, surf the Internet, and send and receive email. The challenge is to find ways to integrate those interests into classroom instruction to motivate students to use reading and writing to learn about and communicate academic content [64, 93].

For struggling readers and writers, this natural decline in motivation is compounded by the grading and grouping practices prevalent in middle and high schools [34, 82]. Grading information (i.e., teacher-assigned grades on assignments and classroom assessments) becomes more important, specific, and pervasive. Grading information is used to make placement decisions, retention and promotion decisions, and as criteria for graduation. Adolescents realize that expectations have changed from mastering a subject or skill to performing well in comparison with others. They are also often tracked with students of similar ability for longer periods of time. At the same time, adolescents experience increased tendencies to compare themselves with their peers. Struggling readers and writers understand more fully that receiving lower grades and being grouped with peers of similar ability and background means that they are perceived as less capable than other students. As adolescents pay more attention to these comparisons, confidence in their abilities and motivations may decline [93].

How Can Instruction Help Adolescent Students with Motivation?

Despite many teachers' beliefs that they have little influence on student motivation, teachers can influence and support student motivation by setting clear goals and expectations (setting a purpose) for reading and writing assignments, focusing students on their own improvement, providing a variety of reading materials, allowing students to choose reading materials, and providing opportunities for students to discuss reading and writing tasks with one another [92, 93, 95].

Set Clear Goals and Expectations for Performance

Adolescents' understanding of a task and the work necessary to complete it successfully influence their motivation [92, 93]. If a teacher assigns a chapter to read for homework without letting the students know that they are expected to discuss the major developments in the chapter the next day, then students do not understand the "real" assignment, nor do they know how to complete it successfully. Goals and expectations for reading and writing assignments should be clear and specific. For example, in assigning a textbook chapter for reading, the teacher should be clear about why the reading is assigned and what students are expected to do as a result of reading it. Provide guidance by giving examples of strategies that students can use in reading the chapter and relate that to successful participation in the discussion to enhance motivation for performing the reading activity [92, 93].

Teachers may feel reluctant to implement the following strategies because of concerns over the relevance of materials that are not directly tied to the curriculum or to high stakes tests. However, if selected in a thoughtful and informed manner, the use of additional materials can provide more students with access to the curriculum and with opportunities to improve their literacy skills. Because high stakes tests are written exams, students must be able to read and write well to succeed. Providing students with activities and materials that can motivate them to improve their content knowledge and their literacy skills has the potential to facilitate struggling adolescents' performance on high stakes tests [92, 93].

Guide Students to Focus on Their Own Improvement

Adolescents' tendencies to compare themselves with their peers, which is exacerbated by grading and tracking practices at the secondary level, negatively influence their motivation for reading and writing in school [92, 93]. Helping students to set goals for their literacy and content learning and then guiding them to focus on their progress toward attaining these goals is one way to improve motivation. In this era of standards-based learning and high stakes testing, teachers must also ensure that individual learning goals address content and performance standards.

Together, the reading specialist, the special education teacher, the school librarian, and content-area teachers can collect and organize a pool of reading materials that address standardsbased content and are written at different reading levels. Specialists can also assist the contentarea teachers by providing diagnostic assessment information and helping them use that information to match texts to students and to determine reading strategies and skills students need to learn. Teachers can then use these resources and information to guide students to set learning goals individualized to their reading abilities and content learning needs and track their progress in meeting these goals. Teachers can teach students to keep track of their progress through reading logs and progress checklists, which the student then shares with the teacher on a regular basis [92].

Provide Variety and Choice in Reading Materials
The textbooks used in many secondary level classrooms often do not hold students' interests. Teachers can provide students with other reading materials that interest them and that pertain to the subjects that they teach. Teachers can start by conducting online searches for *high interest, matched-to-reading-level materials*. Books, magazines, and newspaper articles that adolescents consider interesting help them view reading as a way to learn more about topics that are attractive to them [34, 64, 92].

Self-determination is critical to motivation. Allowing students to select some of their own reading materials gives students control over their learning. Teachers need to structure and guide student choices so that struggling readers select materials that are appropriate for their reading level and that address the content they are learning [92, 93, 95].

Provide Opportunities for Students to Interact through Reading
To provide students with opportunities for interaction, teachers can:

- Create opportunities for small groups of students to discuss their reading,
- Structure groups carefully so that students with differing abilities are able to talk about a common topic, and
- Offer different viewpoints or information on that topic [8, 92].

For example, if students are reading different materials at different reading levels on the writing of the U.S. Constitution, students who have read different selections can form a group to talk about what they learned from the different texts.

What Do We Still Need to Know?

Additional research is needed on the types of cognitive and developmental processes students experience to motivate them to read and learn. Teachers need a better understanding of the characteristics that they should possess to motivate students at higher levels. It may also be important to gain greater insight into what motivating factors must be recognized and taken into account in attempting to measure literacy skills for linguistically or culturally diverse students [95]. These research areas can shed more light on the link between motivation and adolescent literacy levels.

THE NEEDS OF DIVERSE LEARNERS

Adolescents who come to school from diverse family backgrounds, with learning disabilities, or with diverse cultural, linguistic, or socioeconomic backgrounds and who have also fallen behind in their literacy development will benefit from the strategies addressed throughout this report. Many of these students, however, may also need additional support in learning both content and literacy. It is important for teachers to understand differences in students' prior knowledge, skills, and experiences; differences in language or dialect; and differences in cognitive ability. Classroom teachers must seek out their colleagues in special education, bilingual and English as a second language education, and specialists in reading development to understand the backgrounds and abilities of the students they teach. These specialists may recommend modifications or adaptations for particular students.

Specialists may also recommend strategies that support many diverse learners. These strategies include ensuring that diverse learners have opportunities to access prior knowledge and discussing experiences relevant to the topic or content area. Teachers should help students connect what they already know and have experienced to new material. Because diverse learners' knowledge and experiences vary more than those of students who have more homogenous backgrounds, additional time is needed to explore differences and make connections. At times it may be difficult for teachers to understand where a student is coming from; however, it is important not to dismiss students' ideas.

To address the needs of diverse learners, teachers can integrate the following suggestions and strategies into their instruction:

- Present text, ideas, and strategies in different ways. For example, when teaching steps for using a comprehension strategy, say the steps, write the steps, visually represent the steps, and repeat the steps [100].
- Break down literacy and content instruction into smaller chunks than you typically might. Provide more guidance and support when developing skills and strategy use and allow more time for practice [100].

- Provide extended talk time, particularly for those who are learning English or who speak a non-standard dialect of English. Provide opportunities for diverse learners to report orally about group or partner discussions. For example, include partner and small group discussions in your instructional delivery. Monitor the groups to ensure that all students participate [101].
- Model and provide instruction in academic English [101].
- Talk with students individually, asking them questions about what they are learning and encouraging them to explain and clarify their thoughts with you [101].

CONCLUSION

Countless middle and high school students at every socioeconomic level are struggling with learning academic content because they cannot read and write at grade level. To address this problem, all educators, including content-area teachers, need information on how to incorporate effective literacy learning strategies into the content-area curriculum. This document has presented, summarized, and discussed the relevant literature on adolescent literacy and has described promising, research-based instructional practices for improving adolescent literacy skills. Though the research base on adolescent literacy is incomplete, existing research offers some suggestions for how content-area teachers can work with struggling adolescent readers in their classrooms.

Some common themes have emerged from the research literature as effective practices for instruction. The most common suggestion made throughout the research surveyed is that teachers should use systematic, explicit, and direct instruction. When students experience explicit instruction on a specific skill, teacher modeling, guided practice, and independent practice, they are much more likely to become proficient at the skill being taught [12, 28, 35, 75, 83]. The second common theme throughout many of the literacy components discussed is the use of repetition. One way to ensure that students retain a strategy or skill is to review it in different contexts and with different texts [6, 16, 20]. Whether applied to reading a text repeatedly to improve fluency or practicing the steps of a strategy multiple times to master that strategy, repetition contributes to the improvement of adolescent literacy skills.

The improvement of adolescent literacy is an issue that all middle and high school teachers should be equipped to address in their instruction. To be effective, content-area teachers, must be aware of instructional approaches and strategies that can be used within their existing curricula to help improve the literacy levels of the struggling readers that they encounter. In this way, they will learn the content area. We hope that this report provides some of the information needed to help teachers better educate today's adolescents.

REFERENCES

[1]   National Institute of Child Health and Human Development, *Report of the National Reading Panel. Teaching children to read: An evidence-based assessment of the scientific research literature on reading and its implications for reading instruction.* 2004, Government Printing Office: Washington, DC.* http://www.nationalreadingpanel.org.

[2]   Cooper, H. M. & (1998). *Synthesizing research: A guide for literature review. 3rd ed.*, Thousand Oaks, CA: Sage.

[3]   Creswell, J. W. & (2003). Research design: Qualitative, quantitative, and mixed method approaches. 2nd ed., Thousand Oaks, CA: Sage.

[4]   Tierney, R. J. & Shanahan, T. (1991). Research on the reading-writing relationship: Interactions, transactions, and outcomes, in *Handbook of reading research*, R. Barr, et al., Editors. Longman: New York. p. 246-280.

[5]   Moore, D. W., et al. (1999). *Adolescent literacy: A position statement for the Commission on Adolescent Literacy of the International Reading Association*, Newark, DE: International Reading Association. 3.

[6]   Kamil, M. & (2003). Adolescents and literacy: Reading for the 21st century, Washington, DC: Alliance for Excellent Education.*

[7]   Ehren, B., Lenz, K. & Deshler, D. (2004). *Enhancing literacy proficiency with adolescents and young adult, in Handbook of language and literacy,* C. Stone, et al., Editors. Guilford Press: New York.*

[8]   Strickland, D. S. & D. E. (2004). Alvermann, *Learning and teaching literacy in grades 4-12: Issues and challenges, in Bridging the literacy achievement gap, grades 4-12*, D.S. Strickland and D.E. Alvermann, Editors. Teachers College Press: New York. p. 1-13.*

[9]   Hoover, W. A. (2002). The importance of phonemic awareness in

learning to read. *SEDL Letter, 14(3):* p. 9-12.

[10] Torgesen, J. (2004). *Lessons learned from research on interventions for students who have difficulty learning to read, in The voice of evidence in reading research,* P. McCardle and V. Chhabra, Editors. Paul H. Brookes Publishing: Baltimore, MD.*

[11] Bhattarya, A. & Ehri, L. (2004). Graphosyllabic analysis helps adolescent struggling readers read and spell words. *Journal of Learning Disabilities, 37*: p. 331-348.*

[12] Shaywitz, S. E., et al. (1999). Persistence of dyslexia: The Connecticut longitudinal study at adolescence. *Pediatrics, 104*: p. 1351-1359.*

[13] Liberman, I. Y. & Shankweiler, D. (1991). *Phonology and beginning to read: A tutorial, in Learning to read: basic research and its implications,* L. Rieben and C.A. Perfetti, Editors. Lawrence Erlbaum Associates: Hillsdale, NJ.

[14] Shaywitz, S. E., *Dyslexia.* (1996). *Scientific American,. 275:* p. 98-104.

[15] Wagner, R. K. & Torgesen, J. (1987). The nature of phonological processing and its causal role in the acquisition of reading skills. *Psychological Bulletin,. 101*: p. 192-212.

[16] Curtis, M. E. (2004). Adolescents who struggle with word identification: Research and practice, in *Adolescent literacy research and practice,* T.L. Jetton and J. A. Dole, Editors. The Guilford Press: New York. p. 119-134.*

[17] Curtis, M. E. & Chmelka, M. B. (1994). Modifying the Laubauch way to reading program for use with adolescents with LDs. *Learning Disabilities: Research and Practice, 9*: p. 38-43.

[18] Moats, L. C. (2001). When older kids can't read. *Educational Leadership,. 58(6)*: p. 36-40.

[19] Leach, J., Scarborough, H. & Rescorla, L. (2003). Late-emerging reading disabilities. *Journal of Educational Psychology, 95*: p. 211-224.

[20] Archer, A., Gleason, M. & Vachon, V. (2003). Decoding and fluency: Foundation skills for struggling older readers. *Learning Disability Quarterly, 26*: p. 89-101.*

[21] Bertelson, P., et al. (1989). Metaphonological abilities of adult illiterates: New evidence of heterogeneity. *European Journal of Cognitive Psychology, 1(3):* p. 239-250.

[22] Greenberg, D., Ehri, L. C. & Perin, D. (1997). Are word-reading processes the same or different in adult literacy students and third-fifth graders matched for reading level? *Journal of Educational Psychology, 89(2)*: p. 262-275.

[23] Scliar-Cabral, L., et al. (1997). The awareness of phonemes: So close-so far away. *International Journal of Psycholinguistics, 13(38)*: p. 211-240.

[24] Bailey, A. L. & Butler, F. A.(2003). *An evidentiary framework for operationalizing academic language for broad application to K-12 education: A design document.* CRESST/University of California, Los Angeles: Los Angeles.

[25] Schleppegrell, M. (2001). Linguistic features of the language of schooling. *Linguistics and Education, 12(4)*: p. 431-459.

[26] Blevins, W. (2001). *Teaching phonics and word study in the intermediate grades,* New York: Scholastic.

[27] Curtis, M. E. & Longo, A. M. (1999). *When adolescents can't read: Methods and materials that work,* Cambridge, MA: Brookline Books.

[28] Snow, C. E., Burns, M. S. & Griffin, P. (1998). eds. *Preventing reading difficulties in young children,* National Academies Press: Washington, DC.

[29] Foorman, B. R., et al. (1998). The role of instruction in learning to read: Preventing reading failure in at-risk children. *Journal of Educational Psychology, 90*: p. 37-55.

[30] Juel, C. & Minden-Cupp, C. (2000). Learning to read words: Linguistic units and instructional strategies. *Reading Research Quarterly, 35:* p. 458-492.

[31] Curtis, M.E. and L. McCart, *Fun ways to promote poor readers' word recognition.* Journal of Reading, 1992. **35**: p. 398-399.

[32] Moats, L.C., *Efficacy of a structured, systematic language curriculum for adolescent poor readers.* Reading & Writing Quarterly, 2004. **20**(2): p. 145-159.

[33] Graham, S., Harris, K. R. & Loynachan, C. (1993). The basic spelling vocabulary list. *Journal of Educational Research, 86*: p. 363-368.

[34] National Academy of Sciences. (2003). *Engaging schools: Fostering high school students' motivation to learn,* The National Academies Press: Washington, DC.*

[35] Nokes, J. D. & Dole, J. A. (2004). *Helping adolescent readers through explicit strategy instruction, in Adolescent literacy research and practice,* T.L. Jetton and J.A. Dole, Editors, The Guilford Press: New York. p. 162-182.*

[36] Partnership for Reading. (2005). *Put reading first: The research building blocks of reading instruction (2nd ed).* 2003, Retrieved May 1, from http://www.nifl.gov/partnershipforreading/publications/PFRbooklet.pdf.

[37] Mory, E. (1996). Feedback research, in *Handbook of research for*

educational communications and technology, D.H. Jonassen, Editor, Simon & Schuster MacMillan: New York. p. 919-956.

[38] Brice, R. (2004). Connecting oral and written language through applied writing strategies. *Intervention in School and Clinic, 40*: p. 38-47.

[39] Carlisle, J. (2004). Morphological processes that influence learning to read, in *Handbook of language and literacy: Development and disorders*, C.A. Stone, et al., Editors, The Guilford Press: New York.

[40] Nagy, W., Berninger, V. & Abbott, R. (2006). Contributions of morphology beyond phonological to literacy outcomes of upper elementary and middle-school students. *Journal of Educational Psychology, 98*: p. 134-147.

[41] Tolman, C. (2005). Working smarter, not harder: What teachers of reading need to know and be able to teach. *Perspectives, 21*: p. 15-23.

[42] Henry, M. (2005). Spelling instruction in the upper grades: The etymology/morphology connection. *Perspectives, 31*: p. 30-32.

[43] Green, L., et al. (2003). Morphological development in children's writing. *Journal of Educational Psychology, 95*: p. 752-761.

[44] Joshi, R. & Aaron, P. (2005).Spelling: Its development, assessment, instruction, and the science of it. *Perspectives, 31*: p. 1-4.

[45] Carlisle, J. & Stone, C. A. (2005). Exploring the role of morphemes in word reading. *Reading Research Quarterly, 40*: p. 428-447.

[46] RAND, *Reading for understanding: Toward an R&D program in reading comprehension.* 2002, RAND: Santa Monica, CA.*

[47] Calfee, R. C. & Piontkowski, D. C. (1981). The reading diary: Acquisition of decoding. *Reading Research Quarterly, 16*: p. 346-373.

[48] Cunningham, A.E. and K.E. Stanovich, *What reading does for the mind.* American Educator, 1998. *22*: p. 8-15.

[49] Fuchs, L. S., Fuchs, D. & Maxwell, L. (1988). The validity of informal reading comprehension measures. *Remedial and Special Education, 9*: p. 20-29.

[50] Meyer, M. S. & Felton, R. H. (1999). Repeated reading to enhance fluency: Old approaches and new directions. *Annals of Dyslexia, 49*: p. 283-306.

[51] Chall, J. S. (1996). *Stages of reading development.* New York: McGraw-Hill.

[52] Hasbrouck, J. E., Ihnot, C. & Rogers, G. H. (1999). *Read Naturally: A strategy to increase oral reading fluency.* Reading Research and Instruction, 39: p. 27-37.

[53] Harris, R. E., Marchand-Martella, N. & Martella, R. C. (2000). Effects

of a peer-delivered Corrective Reading program. *Journal of Behavioral Education, 10*: p. 21-36.

[54] Allinder, R. M., et al. (2001). Improving fluency in at-risk readers and students with learning disabilities. *Remedial and Special Education, 22(1):* p. 48-54.

[55] Chall, J. S. & Curtis, M. E. (1987). What clinical diagnosis tells us about children's reading. *Reading Teacher, 40*: p. 784-788.

[56] Bryant, D., et al. (2003). Vocabulary instruction for students with learning disabilities: A review of the research. *Learning Disability Quarterly, 26*: p. 117-128.*

[57] Medo, M. & Ryder, R. (1993). The effects of vocabulary instruction on readers' ability to make causal connections. *Reading Research and Instruction, 33(2)*: p. 119-134.

[58] Snow, C. & Biancarosa, G. (2003). *Adolescent literacy and the achievement gap: What do we know and where do we go from here?*, Carnegie Corporation of New York: New York.*

[59] Lehr, F., Osburn, J. & Hiebert, E. H. (2004). *A focus on vocabulary.* Regional Educational Laboratory at Pacific Resources for Education and Learning.

[60] Santa, C. M. (2004). *Project CRISS: Reading, writing, and learning in the content subjects, in Bridging the literacy achievement gap, grades 4-12*, D.S. Strickland and D.E. Alvermann, Editors. Teachers College Press: New York. p. 183-199.*

[61] Mason, L. (2001). Introducing talk and writing for conceptual change: A classroom study. *Learning and Instruction, 11*: p. 305-329.

[62] Underwood, T. & Pearson, P. D. (2004). Teaching struggling adolescent readers to comprehend what they read, in *Adolescent literacy research and practice*, T.L. Jetton and J.A. Dole, Editors. The Guilford Press: New York. p. 135-161.*

[63] Alvermann, D. E. & Eakle, A. J. (2003). Comprehension instruction: Adolescents and their multiple literacies, in *Rethinking reading comprehension*, A.P. Sweet and C.E. Snow, Editors. The Guilford Press: New York. p. 12-29.*

[64] Moje, E. B. & Hinchman, K. (2004). *Culturally responsive practices for youth literacy learning, in Adolescent literacy research and practice*, T.L. Jetton and J.A. Dole, Editors.: New York. p. 321-350.*

[65] Stahl, S. A. & Shanahan, C. (2004). Learning to think like a historian: Disciplinary knowledge through critical analysis of multiple documents, in *Adolescent literacy research and practice*, T.L. Jetton and J.A. Dole,

Editors. The Guilford Press: New York. p. 94115.*

[66] Snow, C. & Biancarosa, G. (2004). *Reading next: A vision for action and research in middle and high school literacy.* Carnegie Corporation of New York: New York.*

[67] Jetton, T. & Alexander, P. A. (2004). *Domains, teaching, and literacy, in Adolescent literacy research and practice,* T.L. Jetton and J.A. Dole, Editors. The Guilford Press: New York. p. 15-39.*

[68] Asimov, I. (1957). The fun they had, in Earth is room enough. Grafton: Los Angeles.

[69] Graves, M. (2004). Theories & constructs that have made a significant difference in adolescent literacy-But have the potential to produce still more positive benefits, in *Adolescent literacy research and practice*, T. Jetton and J. Dole, Editors. The Guilford Press: New York. p. 433-452.

[70] Deshler, D. D. & Schumaker, J. B. (1988). An instructional model for teaching students how to learn, in *Alternative educational delivery systems: Enhancing instructional options for all students*, J.L. Graden, J.E. Ains, and M.J. Curtis, Editors. National Association of School Psychologists: Washington, D.C.

[71] Palincsar, A. S. (1986). *Reciprocal teaching, in Teaching reading as thinking.* North Central Regional Educational Laboratory: Oak Brook, IL.

[72] Palincsar, A. S. & Brown, A. (1984). Reciprocal teaching of comprehension: Fostering and comprehension monitoring activities. *Cognition and Instruction, 1(2)*: p. 117-175.

[73] Palincsar, A.S. &. Brown, A. L (1985). Reciprocal teaching: Activities to promote read(ing) with your mind., in *Reading, thinking and concept development: Strategies for the classroom*, T.L.H.E.J. Cooper, Editor. The College Board: New York.

[74] Palincsar, A. S. & Klenk, L. J. (1991). Dialogues promoting reading comprehension, in *Teaching advanced skills to at-risk students*, C.C. B. Means, and M. S. Knapp, Editor. Jossey-Bass: San Francisco.

[75] Graham, S. (2005). Strategy instruction and the teaching of writing: A meta-analysis, in *Handbook of writing research*, C. MacArthur, S. Graham, and J. Fitzpatrick, Editors. The Guilford Press: New York.*

[76] Klassen, R. (2002). Writing in early adolescence: A review of the role of self-efficacy beliefs. *Educational Psychology Review, 14*: p. 173-203.*

[77] Afflerbach, P. (2004). Assessing adolescent reading, in *Adolescent literacy research and practice*, T.L. Jetton and J.A. Dole, Editors. The Guilford Press: New York. p. 369-391.*

[78] Kibby, M. (1995). *Practical steps for informing literacy instruction: A*

diagnostic decision making model. Newark, DE: International Reading Association.

[79] Kibby, M. & Scott, L. (2002). Using computer simulations to teach decision making in reading diagnostic assessment for re-mediation. *Reading Online, 6(3).*

[80] Nitko, A. J. (1996). *Educational assessment of students. 2nd ed.* Englewood Cliffs, NJ: Merrill.

[81] Black, P., Harrison, C. & et al. (2004). Working inside the black box: Assessment for learning in the classroom. *Phi Delta Kappan, 86(1):* p. 8-21.

[82] Peterson, C., et al. (2000). *Building reading proficiency at the secondary level.* Southwest Educational Development Laboratory: Austin, TX.

[83] Shanahan, T. (2004). Overcoming the dominance of communication: Writing to think and learn, in *Adolescent literacy research and practice,* T.L. Jetton and J.A. Dole, Editors. The Guilford Press: New York. p. 59-74.*

[84] Buerger, J. R. (1997). *A study of the effect of exploratory writing activities on student success in mathematical problem solving.* Columbia University.

[85] McGee, L. M. & Richgels, D. J. (1990). Learning from text using reading and writing, in *Reading and writing together: New perspectives for the classroom,* T. Shanahan, Editor. Christopher-Gordon: Norwood, MA. p. 145-169.

[86] Wong, B. & Berninger, V. (2004). Cognitive processes of teachers in implementing composition research in elementary, middle, and high school classrooms, in *Handbook of language and literacy,* C. Stone, et al., Editors. Guilford Press: New York.*

[87] Meyer, B. J. F. & Poon, L. W. (2001). Effects of structure strategy training and signaling on recall of text. *Journal of Educational Psychology, 93:* p. 141-159.

[88] Urquhart, V. & McIver, M. (2005).*Teaching writing in the content areas.* Alexandria, VA: ASCD and McREL.

[89] Lindemann, E. (1995). *A rhetoric for writing teachers. 3rd ed. ed.* NY: Oxford University Press.

[90] North Central Regional Educational Laboratory, *Graphic organizers.* n.d., North Central Regional Educational Laboratory.

[91] Morretta, T.M. & Ambrosini, M. (2000). *Practical approaches for teaching reading and writing in middle schools.* Newark, DE: International Reading Association.

[92] Wigfield, A. (2004). Motivation for reading during the early adolescent and adolescent years, in *Bridging the literacy achievement gap, grades 4-12*, D.S. Strickland and D.E. Alvermann, Editors. Teachers College Press: New York. p. 56-69.*

[93] Reed, J. H., et al. (2004). Motivated reader, engaged writer: The role of motivation in the literate acts of adolescence, in *Adolescent literacy research and practice*, T.L. Jetton and J.A. Dole, Editors. 2004, The Guilford Press: New York. p. 251-282.*

[94] Wigfield, A. & Guthrie, J. T. (1997). Relation of children's motivation for reading to the amount and breadth of their reading. *Journal of Educational Psychology, 89*: p. 420-432.

[95] Guthrie, J. & Humenick, N. (2004). Motivating students to read: Evidence for classroom practices that increase reading motivation and achievement, in *The voice of evidence in reading research*, P. McCardle and V. Chhabra, Editors. Paul H. Brookes Publishing: Baltimore, MD.*

[96] Ryan, R. M. & Deci, E. L. (2002). Overview of self-determination theory: An organismic dialectical perspective, in *Handbook of self-determination research*, E.L. Deci and R.M. Ryan, Editors. University of Rochester Press: Rochester, NY. p. 3-33.

[97] Zimmerman, B. J. & Shunk, D. H. (2001). *Self-regulated learning and academic achievement: Theoretical perspectives.* Mahwah, NJ: Lawrence Erlbaum Associates.

[98] Guthrie, J. & Davis, M. H. (2003). Motivating struggling readers in middle school through an engagement model of practice. *Reading and Writing Quarterly, 19*: p. 59-85.

[99] Guthrie, J. T. & Wigfield, A. (2000). Engagement and motivation in reading, in *Handbook of reading research*, M.L. Kamil, et al., Editors. Lawrence Erlbaum Associates: Mahwah, NJ. p. 403-422.

[100] Tomlinson, C. A. (2004). Differentiating instruction: A synthesis of key research and guidelines, in *Adolescent Literacy Research and Practice*, T.L. Jetton and J.A. Dole, Editors. 2004, The Guilford Press: NY. p. 228-248.*

[101] Klingner, J. K. & Vaughn, S. (2004). *Strategies for Struggling Second-Language Readers, in Adolescent Literacy Research and Practice*, T.L. Jetton and J.A. Dole, Editors. The Guilford Press: NY. p. 183-209.*

[102] De La Paz, S. & Graham, S. (2002). Explicitly teaching strategies, skills, and knowledge: Writing instruction in middle school classrooms. *Journal of Educational Psychology, 94*, 687-698.

[103] Bean, T. W. & Steenwyk, F. L. (1984). The effect of three forms of

summarization instruction on sixth graders' summary writing and comprehension. *Journal of Reading Behavior, 16*, 297-306.

ADDITIONAL REFERENCES

August, D. & Shanahan, T. (2006). *Developing language in second-language learners: Report of the national literacy panel on language-minority children and youth.* Mahwah, NJ: Lawrence Erlbaum Associates.

Calhoon, M. B. (2006). Rethinking adolescent literacy instruction. *Perspectives, 32*, 31-35.

Commonwealth of Australia. (2005). *Teaching Reading.*

Graham, S. & Perrin, D. (2007). Writing next: Effective strategies to improve writing of adolescents in middle and high schools – A report to Carnegie Corporation of New York Washington, D.C.: Alliance For Excellent Education.

Short, D., & Fitzsimmons, S. (2007). Double the work: Challenges and solutions to acquiring language and academic literacy for adolescent English language learners – A report to Carnegie Corporation of New York. Washington, DC: Alliance for Excellent Education.

Torgesen, J. K., Houston, D. D., Rissman, L. M., Decker, S. M., Roberts, G., Vaughn, S., Wexler, J., Francis, D. J., Rivera, M. O. & Lesaux, N. (2007). *Academic literacy instruction for adolescents: A guidance document from the Center on Instruction.* Portsmouth, NH: RMC Research Corporation, Center on Instruction.

New Roles in Response to Intervention: Creating Success for Schools and Children. (2006). International Reading Association.

APPENDIX A: THINK ALOUDS

When using "think alouds," display the text either on an overhead projector or computer screen. Then read aloud several paragraphs from the class text. As you read, stop now and then to voice what you are thinking about as you read. The following five strategies for monitoring comprehension can be demonstrated using teacher think alouds.

- Identify the occurrence of a comprehension problem
  "I don't know what this second sentence means."
- Identify the comprehension problem
  "I don't know what the author means by "the matter was not completely digested."
- Restate the difficult sentence or passage.
  "I think 'matter' means the issue or problem. Now if the problem was not digested, that could mean that it wasn't through or over."
- Look back through the text to find information that may provide a clue to the meaning of the difficult sentence or passage.
  "When I look back at the previous paragraph, it talks about the argument between the parents on whether Bonnie should visit her grandmother for the summer, so the "matter" was whether Bonnie should visit her grandmother. That sounds like the best possibility."
- Look forward in the text for information that might help solve the comprehension problem.
  "After reading the next couple of paragraphs, I've learned that the parents aren't talking to each other, and so I know that my guess about the matter not being digested was correct."

Student think alouds are another way that teachers can question and observe students' reading skills and strategies. When students think aloud as they read, they describe the reading strategies that they use to make sense of a text. Asking students to think aloud as they read allows the teacher to uncover the details of students' reading strengths and weaknesses within the context of content-area reading.

APPENDIX B: GRAPHIC AND SEMANTIC ORGANIZERS

SPIDER MAPS

Spider Maps are used to describe a central idea: a thing (a geographic region), process (meiosis), concept (altruism), or proposition with support (experimental drugs should be available to AIDS victims). Key frame questions are: What is the central idea? What are its attributes? What are its functions?

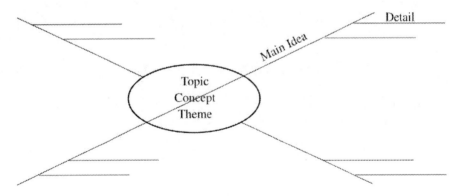

SERIES OF EVENTS CHAINS

Series of Events Chains are used to describe the stages of the steps in a linear procedure (e.g., how to neutralize an acid); a sequence of events (e.g., how feudalism led to the formation of nation states); or the goals, actions, and outcomes of a historical figure or character in a novel (e.g., the rise and fall of Napoleon). Key frame questions include: What is the object, procedure, or initiating event? What are the stages or steps? How do they lead to one another? What is the final outcome?

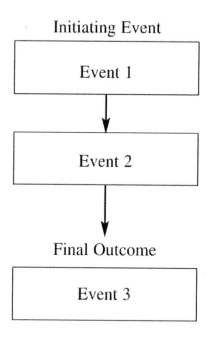

COMPARE/CONTRAST MATRICES

Compare/Contrast Matrices are used to show similarities and differences between two things (people, places, events, ideas, etc.). Key frame questions are: What things are being compared? How are they similar? How are they different?

	Name 1	Name 2
Attribute 1		
Attribute 2		
Attribute 3		

PROBLEM/SOLUTION OUTLINES

Problem/Solution Outlines are used to represent a problem (e.g., the national debt), attempted solutions, and results. Key frame questions include: What was the problem? Who had the problem? Why was it a problem? What attempts were made to solve the problem? Did those attempts succeed?

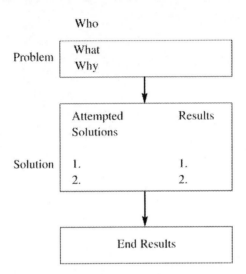

NETWORK TREES

Network Trees are used to represent a problem, attempted solutions, and results (the national debt). Key frame questions: What was the problem? Who had the problem? Why was it a problem? What attempts were made to solve the problem? Did those attempts succeed?

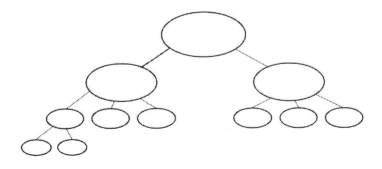

FISHBONE MAPS

Fishbone Maps are used to show the causal interaction of a complex event (e.g., an election, a nuclear explosion) or complex phenomenon (e.g., juvenile delinquency, learning disabilities). Key frame questions include: What are the factors that cause X? How do they interrelate? Are the factors that cause X the same as those that cause X to persist?

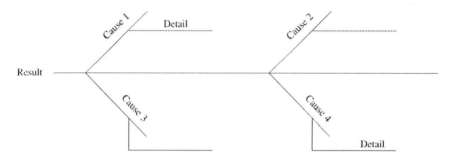

CYCLES

Cycles are used to show how a series of events interact to produce a set of results again and again (e.g., weather phenomena, cycles of achievement and failure, the life cycle). Key frame questions are: What are the critical events in the cycle? How are they related? In what ways are they self-reinforcing?

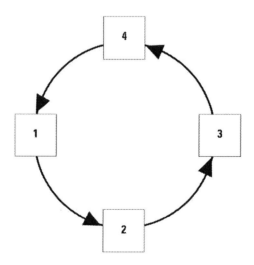

ANTICIPATION/REACTION GUIDES

Anticipation/Reaction Guides are used to assess a class's knowledge before the students begin a lesson. Students respond to each statement about the lesson twice: once before the lesson and again after reading it. The following information about dinosaurs is provided as an example.

Response Before Lesson	TOPIC: Dinosaurs	Response After Lesson
	Dinosaurs are the most successful group of land animals ever to roam the Earth.	
	Paleontology is the study of fossils.	
	Human beings belong to the Zenozoic Era.	
	Most dinosaurs have Greek names.	
	Some dinosaurs are named for places in which their fossilized remains were found.	
	Dinosaurs ruled our planet for over 150 million years.	
	Dinosaurs had small brains	

INQUIRY CHARTS

Inquiry charts are used to examine critical questions by integrating what is already known or thought about a topic with information and ideas obtained from different sources.

	Question Area 1	Question Area 2	Question Area 3	Question Area 4
What I Think				
Source #1				
Source #2				
Source #3				
Summary				

APPENDIX C: EXPLICIT COMPREHENSION STRATEGY INSTRUCTION

Use explicit strategy instruction to make visible the invisible comprehension strategies that good readers use to understand text. Support students until they can use the strategies independently. Recycle and re-teach strategies throughout the year.

PLANNING FOR EXPLICIT STRATEGY INSTRUCTION

After you have chosen a strategy to teach, think about how the strategy works. For example, when good readers monitor their comprehension, they know when they understand, know when they do not understand, and employ problem-solving strategies such as rereading and restating a difficult passage in their own words when they do not understand. Collect several passages from reading materials that you are using in your classroom. Assess the passages for opportunities to model the comprehension strategy. Put these passages on an overhead transparency or slide. Prepare to introduce the strategy, including a description of the strategy, why it is important, and when it should be used.

Teaching Procedures for Explicit Strategy Instruction

Phase 1: Explicit Training and Teacher Modeling

- Activate students' prior knowledge of the topic addressed in your selected passages.
  "Let's look at the title of this chapter and a few of the subheadings. What do you think this passage is going to be about?"
- Name and describe the comprehension strategy you expect students to learn.
  "Good readers monitor their comprehension continuously as they read. We're going to discuss and practice using this strategy to make sure you are using it when you read. When you monitor your comprehension, you frequently ask yourself whether what you are reading makes sense to you. If you decide it doesn't make sense, you stop and figure out what the problem is and how to fix the problem."
- Explain why the strategy helps comprehension and when to use the strategy.
  "We use monitoring comprehension to help us keep track of how well we are understanding what we read. You should use monitoring comprehension while you are reading, particularly when you are reading materials on a topic you don't know much about or if the reading is difficult for you."
- Model or demonstrate how to use the strategy by thinking aloud with the passages you have selected. For visible strategies, such as word mapping or graphic organizers, think aloud about your reasoning processes as you complete the map or organizer.
  Begin reading the passage, pause at several points and ask yourself, "Is this making sense?"
  Next, pause at a place where struggling readers might have difficulty and again ask, "Is this making sense? I'm not sure. I don't know what this second sentence means."
  Identify what the comprehension problem is by saying, "I don't know what the author means by 'the matter was not completely digested.' What was this 'matter,' and why wasn't it 'digested?'"
  Read back over previous sentences that provide clues. Use the clues to make a good guess about what the phrase you don't understand

means. "Maybe the word 'matter' means the argument. I think this is true because the previous paragraph talks about the argument between the parents. Now if the argument was not digested, that could mean that it wasn't done or over. That sounds like the best possibility."
You can also read forward in the text to look for meaning clues.

- Repeat teacher modeling with the other passages.

Phase 2: Guided Practice

- Begin to turn responsibility for the strategy over to the students by providing opportunities for students to practice the strategy with you. For example, after you demonstrate the monitoring comprehension strategy, you can ask individual students to try out reading and thinking aloud.
- Prompt students to pause and ask whether the passage makes sense. Have them check whether it is making sense by occasionally prompting them to summarize or predict.
- Ask students to continue reading and thinking aloud in small groups or pairs. Monitor the groups closely to ensure that they are practicing the strategy, not just reading aloud to one another.

Phase 3: Independent Practice

- Continue turning over responsibility to students by asking them to read independently in class and use the strategies that you have taught.
- Ask students to keep a written log of their strategy use. Periodically ask students to share their logs with the class and lead a discussion about how students are using strategies. For example, have students keep a log of places where they used monitoring comprehension to identify difficulties and the problem-solving strategies that they used to help them overcome the difficulties.
- Continue to support students as they learn new strategies by circulating and reinforcing strategy use on an individual basis.
- Every few weeks, re-teach strategies that you have taught previously and remind students to use them in their reading.

APPENDIX D: RECIPROCAL TEACHING

DESCRIPTION AND PURPOSE

Reciprocal teaching is a "strategy package" that students can use when reading science, social studies, language arts, mathematics, or any other content-area texts. With reciprocal teaching, students learn to use the following four interrelated strategies.

- *Questioning:* Generating questions about the text;
- *Clarifying:* Clearing up confusion about words, phrases, or concepts by using the text as much as possible;
- *Summarizing:* Describing the "gist" of what has been read and discussed; and
- *Predicting:* Suggesting what might be learned from the next part of the text or what will happen next.

Reciprocal teaching is designed to improve students' ability to monitor their comprehension and to learn from their reading. The goal of reciprocal teaching is to help students apply the strategies on their own. Research indicates that with extensive practice, students will master reciprocal teaching strategies and will use them independently for other reading assignments.

Teaching Contexts

Reciprocal teaching can be used with content-area reading material that is extended text.

Target Students

Reciprocal teaching assists all students to become better, more strategic readers.

Teaching Tips

When you first introduce your students to reciprocal teaching, use explicit strategy instruction (instructions are included in this appendix):

- Explain the four strategies,
- Model the strategies,
- Monitor students' learning and understanding,
- Support their efforts to use the strategies, and
- Provide feedback.

As soon as possible, have individual students take turns as the class leader. As you gradually turn over responsibility to the students, continue to monitor individuals as they read, keep small groups focused on strategy use, and facilitate use of the strategies.

PROCEDURES

Teacher-directed Phase

As the leader, begin by reading aloud a short passage from classroom text or other material that students are currently reading. Then follow steps one through four below.

1. *Question the Text:* After reading the short passage aloud, generate several questions prompted by the text. Questions should focus on

main ideas, not discrete facts. Encourage students to answer the
questions.

2. *Clarify the Text:* If there are any problems with or misunderstandings
   of the text, clarify them. Encourage students to help you clarify these
   problems and misunderstandings.

3. *Summarize the Text:* When all questions and clarifications have been
   addressed, summarize the passage. Encourage students to help you
   summarize the passage.

4. *Predict the Text:* Based on the passage just read, previously read
   passages, and the discussion generated in steps 1-3, make predictions
   about the content of the next passages. Encourage students to help you
   make predictions.

Repeat this sequence of reading, questioning, clarifying, summarizing, and
predicting with several more passages.

Student-directed Phase

Ask for volunteers from the class to take on the role of the leader. Guide
them through the four steps outlined above. When students are ready, divide
the class into small groups. Students who have assumed the role of the leader
can be assigned to each small group to lead that group through the four steps.
Monitor the groups closely to ensure that all students take turns using each
strategy. Eventually all students will lead their group and use all four
strategies.

APPENDIX E: WORD MAP

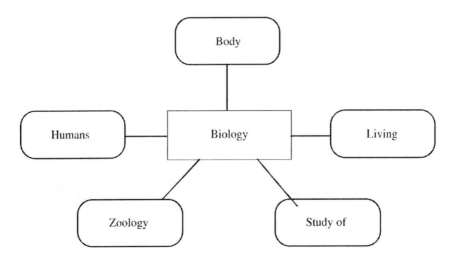

APPENDIX F: THE PLAN AND WRITE STRATEGY

Use strategy instruction to teach students to plan, revise, and edit their compositions. This instruction is explicit and systematic. PLAN helps students to analyze the demands of a writing assignment. It specifically helps to generate and organize possible writing content [102]. It is important to model how to use the writing strategy, to provide extensive instruction and practice, and to provide assistance until the strategy becomes automatic and the student can apply the strategy independently.

Teach Procedures for the Planning Strategy – PLAN

- P – *P*ay attention to the prompt
- L – *L*ist main ideas
- A – *A*dd supporting ideas
- N – *N*umber your ideas

Teach Procedures for the Writing Strategy – WRITE

- W – Work from your plan to develop your thesis statement
- R – Remember your goals
- I – Include transition words, for each paragraph
- T – Try to use different kinds of sentences
- E – Exciting, interesting, $100,000 words

APPENDIX G: SUMMARIZATION STRATEGY

Use direct instruction to teach students a rule-based strategy to summarize paragraph-length material [103] and carefully guide students through each step with the use of teacher modeling. Instructors should apply this with the whole group and with small groups and provide feedback. Then, have students practice these skills and follow-up with individual application.

There are two summarization strategies that have been found to be effective. One is the rulegoverned approach and the other is the GIST approach.

Strategy One – Rule-governed Approach

The rule-governed approach

- Delete unnecessary or trivial material
- Delete material that is important, but redundant
- Substitute a superordinate term for a list of items
- Substitute a superordinate term for components of an action
- Select a topic sentence
- When there is no topic sentence, invent one

Strategy Two – GIST (Generating Interaction between Schemata and Text) Approach

The GIST approach

- Student is given an article to summarize
- The length of the student's summary is limited to 15 words.
- As the student reads subsequent paragraphs of an article, the student must intuitively delete trivial propositions and select the macro level idea. Thinking about *who, what, when, where*, and *how* may help with this.
- Student must select topic statements to fit the 15 – blank word limit

INDEX

reading difficulties, 7, 13, 39, 44, 61
reading skills, 8, 10, 41, 43, 46, 60, 70
reasoning, 35, 78
reasoning skills, 35
recall, 65
recognition, 6, 16, 21, 22, 61
regular, 19, 31, 48, 54
regulation, 46, 49, 50, 51
relationship, 6, 10, 17, 21, 24, 26, 50, 59
relationships, 15, 26, 34
relevance, 53
repetitions, 26
resources, 1, 35, 53
retention, 26, 52
rhetoric, 65
rhythm, 23
risk, 61, 63, 64
rubrics, 43, 47, 49

S

sample, 31, 37
school, xi, xii, 1, 2, 5, 6, 7, 8, 13, 15, 17, 19,
  20, 23, 29, 32, 40, 44, 49, 52, 53, 55, 57,
  61, 62, 64, 65, 66, 67
schooling, 61
search, xii
search terms, xii
searches, xii, 54
searching, 23
second language, 55
secondary teachers, 39
segmentation, 7, 9
selecting, 10, 24, 38
self-determination theory, 66
self-efficacy, 50, 64
self-monitoring, 46
self-regulation, 46, 49, 50
semantic, 10, 34, 35
sensitivity, 19, 22, 44
sentences, 17, 21, 22, 25, 26, 78, 87
services, viii
sexism, 11
shape, xii, 48
shares, 44, 54

sharing, 49
signaling, 65
simulations, 65
skills, xi, xii, 1, 2, 5, 6, 7, 8, 9, 10, 12, 13,
  16, 17, 22, 23, 24, 27, 29, 35, 40, 41, 42,
  43, 44, 45, 46, 47, 48, 49, 51, 53, 55, 57,
  60, 64, 66, 70, 89
socioeconomic, 2, 55, 57
socioeconomic background, 3, 55
software, 28
sounds, 6, 7, 8, 9, 18, 22, 69, 79
special education, 20, 44, 45, 53, 55
speech, 1, 7, 15, 21, 22, 26
speed, 16, 17
spelling, 6, 11, 14, 16, 17, 46, 61
sponsor, xi
sports, 33
stages, 17, 71
standards, 41, 49, 53
strategy use, 36, 42, 51, 55, 79, 82
stress, 49
student achievement, 5
student motivation, 2, 52
subtasks, 51
summaries, 36
summer, 69
supplemental, 38
syntactic, 22, 27
syntax, 21, 23
synthesis, xi, 31, 66

T

teacher preparation, 43
teachers, viii, xii, 1, 2, 3, 5, 7, 10, 11, 12,
  14, 15, 16, 19, 20, 24, 25, 27, 30, 31, 32,
  34, 36, 37, 38, 40, 41, 42, 43, 44, 45, 46,
  47, 48, 49, 52, 53, 54, 55, 57, 62, 65, 70
teaching, 1, 3, 5, 10, 11, 12, 14, 15, 24, 25,
  26, 30, 36, 42, 47, 55, 59, 64, 65, 66, 81,
  82
teaching strategies, 66, 81
textbooks, 14, 15, 54
thinking, 12, 32, 36, 37, 42, 64, 69, 78, 79
title, 33, 78

tracking, 53
training, 36, 43, 65
transactions, 59
transcription, 17
transfer, 29
transition, 34, 87
transparency, 77

V

validity, 62
values, 50, 51
variance, 5
victims, 71
visible, 77, 78
vision, 45, 64
vocabulary, xii, 2, 5, 8, 9, 10, 11, 12, 14, 16,
19, 21, 22, 23, 24, 25, 26, 27, 28, 45, 50,
61, 63

voice, 60, 66, 69

W

word meanings, 23, 25, 26
word recognition, 6, 21, 61
working groups, xii
workplace, 43, 49
writing, xi, xii, 1, 2, 12, 13, 17, 21, 25, 26,
29, 39, 41, 43, 46, 47, 48, 49, 50, 51, 52,
53, 54, 59, 62, 63, 64, 65, 67, 87
writing process, 17, 46, 47, 48, 49
writing tasks, 1, 50, 51, 52

Y

youth literacy, 63